The Last Garden
A Memoir

For Claudia – with
gratitude for your own
beautiful art and in
celebration of your love
of gardens – I hope we
meet in person, soon!
♡

14 May 2021

LIZA KETCHUM

*The transgression of Eve was an act of courage
that led us out of the garden and into the wilderness.
Who wants to be a goddess when we can be human?*
—Terry Tempest Williams
When Women Were Birds

To the gardeners in my life,

past and present, who shared their gifts and knowledge

as we cultivated, weeded, pruned, transplanted

and talked about plants, through the seasons:

My love and gratitude.

Table of Contents

Table of Contents
(continued)

Part One
Sowing the Seeds

A writer who gardens is sooner or later going to write a book about the subject.
—Eleanor Perényi
Green Thoughts: A Writer in the Garden

Plants have an ability that no animal does: they can,
theoretically, live forever.
—William Cullina
Native Trees, Shrubs, and Vines

Timothy

Phleum pratense

The first garden is a meadow.

I am four years old, gripping the crosspieces of a hay wagon. It creaks and sways as a pair of Belgians lean into their harnesses, pulling us up the steep hillside. The fragrance of new-mown hay curing in the sunshine tickles my nostrils. The scent mingles with the smell of horse piss, sweat and the smoke from Hope Hazelton's cigarette, dangling from a corner of her mouth. Above us, the lip of the hayfield curves beneath the blue sky like the rim of a teacup.

The huge horses are the color of butterscotch. Their massive shoulders ripple. Their tails flick through clouds of flies on their rumps. Their hooves, big as dinner plates, could crush me in an instant, but I'm not afraid. I lean back against Hope's sturdy legs as she drives the team. I chew on a stalk of timothy, imitating Hope and her cigarette.

Hope wears overalls, the denim so worn it's almost white. Her hands—deeply grooved, with swollen knuckles—cup the reins. The team responds to her slightest touch, as if she were connected to their velvet muzzles. I know the feel of those muzzles, because Hope once lifted me so I could touch the soft skin around their nostrils. The delicate hair tickled my fingertips.

"Back, you Babe!" she calls to the lead horse. The team jerks to a halt and I almost lose my balance. Hope's husband, Linwood, and their daughter, Patty, fork hay from raked rows into the wagon bed, then climb into the wagon where they stomp on it, jouncing up and down like clumsy dancers.

Hope nudges my shoulder. I look up. Her eyes twinkle. Her gray curls, wet with sweat, are plastered to her forehead. "Want to drive?" she asks.

I nod. She grabs me under my armpits and settles my feet on her knees; pulls me back against her body and gives me the reins. I wrap my small fingers around the wide leather traces. Hope clucks to the team. The Belgians surge, their power coursing into my arms like an electric current. The thrust of their weight yanks me forward as they lean into the hill.

When we reach the stone wall at the top of the meadow, the Belgians stop to blow and a bird flies up out of the grass, wings beating. "Meaderlark," Hope says. "Could be we disturbed her nest."

I look down the steep hill. My whole world lies below: our white house with its slate roof; the henhouse where "my girls"—as I call our chickens—lay their eggs. The weeping elm that trails its branches into the Mettawee River. With a thrill, I realize that I'm higher than my house, higher even than my tall, lanky father.

This is the only world I know. I've never been out of Vermont and I'm too young to understand the circle of life in this hayfield. Thanks to the small farms on our road, I know that the hay in the wagon feeds the horses through the winter. But do I understand that the hot manure plopping in front of us fertilizes this field? Or that the litter from Hope and Linwood's chicken house nourishes their vegetable garden? Or that the trees they've cut in the woodlot, just beyond the wall, will fuel their woodstove this winter?

Probably not. I'm too young. Hope and Linwood seem old, like my grandmother (who is only fifty). Yet this is where my love of open land begins, in the beauty of a pasture, bordered on all sides by stone walls tucked up against the woods. Years later, I will learn about the backbreaking labor that converted thick forests into hayfields. I will see paintings of men cutting massive trees with a two-man saw, wrestling stones from the ground onto a stone boat pulled by a team of oxen. I haven't yet learned the names of the trees that will become my life-long friends and companions: elm, oak, hop hornbeam; beech, butternut, ironwood. The birches: white, gray, yellow, paper and river. And the conifers: hemlock, balsam, white pine, red and blue spruce. The majestic tulip tree. Shagbark hickory. The maples: red, striped and (my favorite) sugar maple. And last but not least, the fruit trees: apple, pear, plum, cherry.

The field seems enormous as the wagon climbs to the inverted bowl of the sky. My world is one of scented grass, green hills, obedient animals, seasonal chores, kind neighbors. An Eden.

Many years ago, Horace wrote: "This is what I prayed for, a piece of land not so very large, where there is a garden, and near the house an ever-flowing spring of water, and above this a bit of woodland." The love of the soil, an urge to make it bear fruit, is a part of the heritage of most of us, whether we be city bred or transplanted there, or dwellers in the country.

—Sam Ogden
Step-by-Step to Organic Vegetable Gardening

Asparagus

Asparagus officionalis

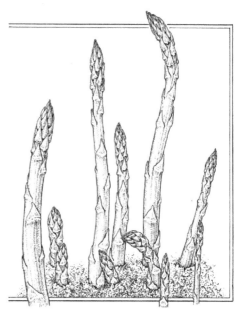

In June of 2012, my husband John and I buy a Vermont farmhouse, a few miles from Hazelton's meadow and my childhood home. John falls in love with the house on our first visit. We both admire its small rooms, the sunshine pouring in the windows, and the beautiful painted mural of Audubon birds on the dining room wall, which inspires our grandson to call our new home The Birdhouse. I'm drawn immediately to the yard and its gardens. The half-acre lot is overgrown. A straggly yew looks as if it is about to swallow the garage; a spirea (*not* my favorite shrub) knocks against a living room window; tall weeds and Jerusalem artichokes choke a former vegetable garden.

But the property has all the elements mentioned by Horace—a garden near the house and a well so copious that its overflow feeds a pond across the road. Horace's "bit of woodland" is actually a healthy sugarbush on the far side of a field. Even better, the tangled garden boasts an asparagus bed. No matter that chest-high weeds cramp the feathery foliage. Someone else cut the sod, dug the bed, sifted the soil to free it from stones, spread the roots of the delicate crowns, and tended the plants through their early years until the delicious stalks were ready to cut and carry to the steamer.

Treasures lurk in the asparagus jungle. The spent blooms of peonies cling stubbornly to a split-rail fence like sad, after-the-ball corsages. Day lilies and monarda poke through the asparagus fronds. And is that a monkshood, surrounded by goldenrod? Jewelweed and battered clumps of Siberian iris look forlorn beneath the bathroom window, but surely they would thrive if I moved them into the sunshine?

A goldfinch flutters out of the ancient lilac and lands in a majestic sugar maple, while a hummingbird's wings thrum near the kitchen window. A tough wire fence surrounds the entire yard, making it safe for grandkids. Even better, I learn that the previous owner anchored the fence in concrete to keep her dogs from tunneling out of the yard. Could this extravagance keep varmints from digging their way in? (My comeuppance comes the following spring, when rabbits and a fat woodchuck mow down my beets, chard and cucumbers. A skunk waltzes in and out of the garage, and the fiercest of all weasels, a fisher cat, tunnels into our compost after killing a turkey gobbler—*inside* our fence.)

When we decide to purchase the house, I realize this might be my last garden. The thought is both exhilarating and frightening. I turn sixty-six a few days after the closing. I have been gardening—or shaped by gardens—my entire life. Now, at an age where I can see the horizon, this could be the last garden I plan, shape and tend.

John is appalled. "What do you mean: 'The *last* garden?' Are you planning to die soon?" he asks. Of course not. I hope to be like Stanley Kunitz, whose wonderful book of poems and garden musings (*The Wild Braid*) sits on my desk. The subtitle itself is an inspiration: *A Poet Reflects on a Century in the Garden.* With luck, I might have decades of gardening left.

So I buy and label a new garden notebook. I make the first entry, and immediately, unbidden, other gardens in my life appear, as do the gardeners who created them. Like characters in my novels who stick around after a book is finished, demanding another adventure, these gardeners—some long dead, others very much alive—will be with me as I sketch out plans for the new garden, turn the soil, order seeds, experiment with new varieties and nurture the plants I love best. When I deadhead spent flowers, yank at a stubborn burdock, spread manure, swat blackflies at planting time, cut the first lush peonies or harvest vegetables, I hope their wisdom will help me to bring this Last Garden to life.

But why describe fragments of a life through gardens? When I worked with students on their writing, I urged them to find a through line: the emotional thread that pulses beneath their stories like the drone on a bagpipe. For me, the garden has provided that steady hum. As I moved from country to city and back again, from marriage to divorce and remarriage, I always had gardens. The times in my life when I *didn't* have a garden were often fraught and unhappy. My children were born, grew up, left home, married and had children themselves. I made friends, lost them, gained new ones—always against a garden backdrop.

I have knelt in wet soil and wept over the end of a marriage. I have raged at the actions of our government while hacking at a blackberry tangle. I have proudly served tomato sauce in January that I cooked and froze in August; displayed the fruits of a city vegetable garden on the kitchen counter when cousins visited; kissed the ravishing pink petals of a peony that blooms on my birthday; held a toddler grandchild up to breathe in the fragrance of a lilac.

I have gardened at my grandmother's house, at a summer camp in the mountains where we raised organic vegetables, and in a small urban plot. With help, I have carved gardens out of inhospitable soil, in city and country. I planted lettuce near the front door of a rented condo and was roundly scolded by the president of the condo association for breaking the rules. (We had tender lettuce for dinner. He didn't.)

Gardens have been a constant in spite of changes in geography, climate, seasons, soil health and hardiness zones. They have kept me company when loneliness threatened. And they put me in touch with others—most often, but not always, women—who share my love of trees, flowers and vegetables. They bring back memories of my grandparents, my parents and my aunt, all departed. Now, as my grandkids help me sow seeds in the spring and harvest vegetables in summer and fall, my gardens are threaded through five generations.

...though I don't believe in ghosts
I am haunted by lilacs.
—Linda Pastan
"Lilacs"

Lilac

Syringa vulgaris

When my husband and I first learned that the Vermont property was for sale, it seemed meant to be. The house was originally home to the farmer who managed Saddleback Farm's herd of Guernsey cows. My parents bought that farm in the 1960s and tried to keep the dairy going—but after a year of dismal milk prices, and the challenges of running a farm from a distance, they sold the cows at a heartbreaking auction, built themselves a new house on a hill behind the barn, and put the farmhouse on the market. The property passed through a few owners before Edith Snare—a friend of our family—purchased and renovated it. She lived there until her death, as did her daughter, Marjorie Chapman.

Just before he died, I told my father that we might buy the house from Marjorie's estate. Dad gave me a wry smile. "Great!" he said. "I always regretted selling that place." Now the house has come full circle.

The day after we sign the purchase and sale agreement, I cross the road and stand in front of my parents' empty dairy barn, taking in the full view of our new property. The house sits on a half-acre plot. Though much of the yard needs tending, a stately row of sugar maples marks its northern boundary, while another broad-crowned maple shades the front of the house. A split-rail fence runs along the road, separating the yard from the grassy ditch. A tangle of ferns, poison parsnip and bishop's weed chokes two ancient lilacs in need of pruning.

A scrim of memory blurs my vision. Didn't Skidmore's house—hardly more than a shack—sit where the lilac grows now?

I close my eyes. Memory floods in.

I am eight years old, spending the summer at Brook House, my grandmother's home just down the road. On hot days, I ride my mom's old fat-tire bike up the steep hill and onto the flats, past the neighboring Hart farm. The gravel road is rutted, and my legs are too short to use the seat, so I pedal standing up. The bike is a monster, black with an orange stripe. My younger brother Tom and his friends jeer at this old-fashioned clunker, but riding it makes me feel strong and powerful.

The tires shiver on the road's corduroyed surface but I stay upright as I pass the Hart Farm. Their herd of dairy cows—a mix of different breeds—grazes in steep pastures, pockmarked with stones. The Harts live in a worn clapboard house where Colonials stored ammunition during the Revolution. If the milk truck is due, tin milk cans glint in the sun at the end of the Hart's driveway, waiting for pickup.

Rounding the corner, I bump along the straightaway toward the next farm, owned by Mr. Yates, a mysterious man who lives in New York State and has left his farm's management to two brothers, Merwin and Malcolm Wells. Though I don't know it now, this farm is losing money. Someday, it will belong to my parents.

I'm headed for the P Street turnoff, a name whose bathroom humor makes us smirk. (The road, named for three long-ago residents whose names all began with the letter P, eventually takes on the more polite moniker of "Peace" Street.) The centerpiece of the Yates farm is a long white barn on the left side of the road. Two silos loom above the barnyard, where red-brown and white Guernsey cattle graze in the pasture near a stagnant pond. If I pass in the late afternoon, the cows are lined up outside, patiently waiting. When they lumber into the barn, they plod obediently to their assigned stanchions.

The Skidmore family lives across from the barn. Outside their small house, barefoot children carve roads in the dirt with toy trucks, while their father—known to us only as Skidmore—perches on a stool, an old cap pulled low on his forehead. He nurses a bottle and occasionally curses the kids, using words that, my mother says: "Will never touch my mouth."

Every other house I pass boasts a vegetable garden. Hollyhocks bow their heads over rows of beans, peas, tomatoes, sweet corn, squash and onions. Scarecrows shiver in the wind on the back corners, wearing last year's overalls and bleached straw hats. Chickens scratch for bugs in the grass. In Lil Baker's yard, a solitary goat tethered to an iron stake chomps on a multiflora rose. But there's no sign of a garden at Skidmore's. Nothing could grow in that hard-packed dirt.

I'm fascinated and a bit thrilled by this family whose lives are so different from my own. Later, I'm ashamed. How rude and stuck-up I must have seemed to them, staring as I biked past!

Now I'm older than Skidmore was when he died. In college, caricatures of this family showed up in my fiction. My awkward stories reeked of naiveté, as well as my ignorance of rural poverty. It's hard to separate fact from fiction. Did Skidmore, as my father told me, really hike to the marble quarry every day? Was he a powder monkey? If so, did he lose his hearing in the blasts that split the marble into clean slabs? Did he understand that the giant blocks of marble, wrestled from Dorset's quarries and loaded onto rail cars, would become the New York Public Library, Harvard Medical School and the U.S. Supreme Court? Did Skidmore often sleep in his car, as our friend Malc told us?

After my father's death, I find a folder full of interviews that Dad conducted with local farmers. Most were men, but sometimes their wives chimed in. They reminisced about farming in the early decades of the 20th century, before farming was mechanized, and before rural electrification brought our Mettawee River Valley into the modern world. Dad was particularly interested to learn more about Saddleback Farm, the property he purchased in the '60s. Reading through the interviews, I learn the parcel of land where my parents' house now stands—across the road from Skidmore's—was originally the town's Poor Farm. Indigent residents of the town lived there and raised their own food to support themselves and repay their debts. Financial support for the Poor Farm was raised at Town Meeting each year. Was it coincidence or necessity that the Skidmores, who had fallen on hard times, lived across the street from the Poor Farm?

Whatever the case, the Skidmores left reminders behind. More than sixty years since my childhood biking days, two young gardeners arrive on a hot July morning to help me prune the overgrown lilac. As they tug on bishop's weed, tangled in the shrub's skirts, and yank out poison parsnip, a shovel clangs. They pry up pieces of scrap metal: rusted parts of old tools and equipment we can't identify.

Did this lilac take root in Skidmore's time? If so, perhaps it bore silent witness to the family's departure, the destruction of their home. When the weeds are gone, the soil beneath the lilac is dark and full of worms. John and I layer newspaper and cardboard to keep the weeds down, and cover everything with wood chips. The lilac looks tidy, and when it finally blooms the following spring, its flowers are a clean, crisp white against glossy green leaves.

The Skidmore family is gone, but their shades haunt that end of the yard.

An addiction to gardening is genetic.
—Penelope Lively
Dancing Fish and Amonites: A Memoir

Sundrops Primrose

Oenothera fructicosa

A year after we purchase The Birdhouse, its gardens take shape. We have pruned and weeded, discarded invasive plants and uncovered healthy perennials beneath the tangles. We follow design suggestions mapped out by our friend Robin Wilkerson, a master gardener and designer, who sketched out a possible plan for the garden's layout.

On a hot July day, I gather a trowel and bucket and walk the short distance between The Birdhouse and the house my parents built in the 1970s. I'm walking a road that is a ribbon, connecting the earliest gardens of my life. My grandmother's old home, Brook House, is a half mile from

The Birdhouse. A few miles beyond that, in Dorset Hollow, sits a more luxurious version of the crumbling farmhouse that my parents bought for $1,500 in 1945, where I spent my first five years. But my objective today is my parents' nearby yard (now owned by my brother) and their patch of sundrops primrose.

The cheerful, butter-yellow flowers nod in the hot wind. I dig a few clumps for our new garden. As I gently untangle the roots with the trowel and my fingers, I'm transported back to Brook House, where I spent most of my childhood summers. There, primrose grew in abundance on the banks of the brook that bisected my grandmother's property.

As a child, I decided that my grandmother carried the most impressive name in the family: Mary Louise McKelvey Bray Armstrong. She was known as "Weezie," after I tried (and failed) to pronounce her name as a toddler. Weezie called her home Brook House in honor of the small stream and the Mettawee River, which rushed along at the foot of her yard. I thought of these five acres as Weezie's *queendom*. (The word was not in any dictionary, but when I was young, I decided we needed a female equivalent to *kingdom*.) Weezie was definitely the queen during my childhood, while the rest of us—including her second husband, my beloved Grandpa Gil—were her subjects, some more loyal than others.

My grandmother bought Brook House a few years after Tom Bray, her adored first husband, died of a burst appendix. Her reign there continued for almost 30 years. The main house was actually created by the merger of two houses rescued from the town of Enfield, Massachusetts, a community flooded when Quabbin Reservoir was constructed to serve the city of Boston. Thirty of Enfield's original houses were disassembled, board by board and beam by beam, carefully labeled and moved to Dorset, where carpenters put them back together. As a child, I imagined the builders reconstructing Brook House as if they were building with a toy set of smooth wooden blocks. Had someone stitched the two houses together in the middle? I searched, but never found a joining seam.

Weezie lived in what we called The Big House, perched at the top of the hill. The Guest House—where my parents, my brother Tom and I lived during the summer—was halfway down the hill. (Interesting that we were family, yet referred to as "guests." Could we be turned out if someone more interesting showed up?) Later, our parents converted the tool shed that sat above the Mettawee River into The Teensy House, where my friends and I slept on cots and read by flashlight. Privately, I thought of the three houses as Papa Bear, Mama Bear and Baby Bear.

For years, Brook House was our family's summer home. Each spring, I waited for late June, when school finally ended in Bronxville, New York. That's when real life began. After I'd written the last book report, performed at the dreaded piano recital, and said good-bye to my winter friends, I packed my rigid gray suitcase and scooped up Ralph, our heavy tiger cat. I plunked him into a bushel basket, clamped the wire handles over the lid, and set his basket among the coolers, duffel bags and cartons of books in the back of the station wagon. Ralph mewled as the car nosed out of the driveway and headed north. Suburban life evaporated behind me, like a dream that disappears on waking.

If I close my eyes, I can see every room in Weezie's Big House in detail, as if I am navigating a camera dolly, one eye to the lens. I scroll through all four floors, from the dank basement to the first floor, where the cozy pine room's dark paneling, fireplace and corner cupboard full of blue glass, contrasted with the bright sunporch, where Weezie's chintz-covered armchair took center stage. (No one dared sit in this chair, even when she was away.)

A tall, black chair stood at the end of the porch. The chair's right arm ended with a wooden circle just the right size for the telephone. The phone had no dial, just a small paper disk with 135—Weezie's number—written in ink. When we lifted the receiver to make a call, a woman's voice drawled, "Number puh-leeze." (The phone operators worked in a small building next to Peltier's General Store in the village.) As a southpaw, I resented the right-handedness of the chair. And I envied Weezie for her private line. Our guesthouse phone (168W) was a party line. Once, when my friend Sally and I had been chatting too long, the operator interrupted us. "You girls need to stop talking right now," she snapped. "We have an emergency on the other line." I slammed down the phone, ashamed but annoyed. How often did she listen in on our calls?

An enormous vase from Bennington Pottery stood next to the phone chair. Gladiolas filled the vase in late summer. The tall flowers arrived in the back of a station wagon driven by "the glad man." (When I was young, I thought that "glad" referred to his cheery personality, rather than his flowers.) For some reason, perhaps because Weezie didn't grow them herself, his gladiolas seemed phony, ostentatious.

On the second floor, in her bright bedroom filled with curly maple furniture, Weezie ate breakfast in bed: a meal brought to her by an ever-changing parade of cooks. Her bedroom window looked out over the kitchen porch and allowed her to keep track of everyone who came up the walk. A steep third flight of stairs led to the cramped, third floor bedrooms and the creepy attic where bats clung to the triangle-shaped screen under the peak of the roof.

Because I lived outside for most of the summer, Weezie's gardens are even more vivid in my memory. Her gardens felt like outdoor rooms, with their perennials, ferns, trees and shrubs. Weezie's five acres were planned and cultivated. She believed she had total control of the place. However, the Brook House property was big enough that my brother and I, as well as our mother, carved out our own small fiefdoms. We felt subversive claiming these hideouts, but Weezie tolerated our small takeovers.

A stone wall ran along the driveway, and paperwhite birches, graceful as young dancers, leaned over the stream. Maidenhair fern grew in profusion on the shady stream banks, their fronds delicate as spider webs, and primroses blanketed the sunnier sections of the bank with a carpet of lemon-yellow blooms. A narrow white footbridge crossed the brook at a high point, connecting the driveway with the lawn and perennial borders beyond.

Until I went to summer camp, I spent many warm days with my nose in a book. I divided my reading time between three places: a small platform that our father built in the fork of a tree above the Mettawee; a hammock slung between two white pines; and the white footbridge, where I sat on the planking, my feet dangling above the brook. The stream burbled below as I followed Sherlock Holmes in his quest for clues or wept over Black Beauty's miserable treatment. I promised myself that, when I finally had a horse of my own, she would never suffer such abuse. Sadly, Weezie ignored my pleas when the tiny pasture on the other side of the Mettawee came up for sale.

"That field is perfect for a horse," I told her. "And it only costs a thousand dollars." (How did I know this? I must have eavesdropped on my father, who was always interested in property for sale. I now suspect that he dreamed of escaping his mother-in-law's iron rule.)

Weezie dismissed me with a wave, her heavy rings glinting in the sun. "Who's going to pay for the land or buy the horse? And where will it live during the winter? Who will feed it when you're not here?"

"What about Artie?"

"Hah!" Artie, Weezie's gardener, laughed and rolled his eyes when I proposed my plan. A budding artist, he presented me with a miniature painting of a swayback horse standing beneath a tree, as if to ease my pain. Of course, there was no room for a real horse in our small suburban yard outside New York City. Instead, I was stuck playing with my old rocking horse, Mitzy, named for the first horse I ever rode. Mitzy had lost her rocking mechanism long ago, but on flat ground, I could balance her nicely on her four small hooves.

Fifty years later, those memories flood back as I dig up a clump of sundrops primrose at my parents' former house. Given that my relatives are more willing to part with plants than with other possessions, I assume that Mom and Dad probably moved these flowers from Brook House. Now the primrose will have a third home in our new garden. I set them gently in a bucket and carry them to a small bed I've dug against The Birdhouse fence. I heel in the floppy plants, hoping their yellow blooms will hide and soften the metal page wire. I've transplanted a piece of my childhood summers.

The flowers of the garden guide us with their smiles.
—Sidi Abou Madyan (12th Century)
quoted in Naomi Shihab Nye's
The Turtle of Oman

Petunia

Petunia hybrida

Weezie was a flapper in the Roaring Twenties. During Prohibition, she drank gin brewed in the bathtub by her husband Tom Bray, the grandfather I never knew. She smoked cigarettes in tapered holders and danced the Charleston at parties. In a photo from those days, Weezie dances on a table, her feet surrounded by wine and champagne glasses. She wears a short flapper dress and beads, her hair cut in a becoming cloche.

My best friend Sally and I were intimately familiar with Weezie's wardrobe. We spent hours dressing up in her discarded ball gowns. On summer mornings, Sally and I tried on Weezie's dresses in our secret hideout under the weeping elm tree. Still flat-chested, neither one of us could fill her generous smocked bodices. I especially loved Weezie's maroon gown with spaghetti straps (though I had to cinch the straps behind my neck to keep it from falling down), and her black velvet pants and jacket, embossed with enormous pink roses—a jacket I still wear on New Year's Eve. Weezie's feet were small, so we almost fit into her mules and worn sequined pumps.

The more outrageous side of my grandmother wasn't in evidence at Brook House, but she still loved parties. Grandpa Gil understood that she'd never recovered from the loss of my biological grandfather, Tom Bray, who died in 1941 before antibiotics were readily available. Yet flashes of Weezie's more playful personality emerged when her best friend, Lib Adams ("Aunt Lid" to me) came to visit. In one rare photo, she and Lib posed for the camera in faded overalls, their arms full of peonies. Their hats sit at a rakish angle and their sly grins suggest they were up to no good. (Would Sally and I look like this in fifty years?)

In spite of that photo, I have no memory of Weezie actually *working* in the garden. Unlike my paternal grandmother, who was comfortable with garden tools and weeded, hoed and transplanted by the hour, Weezie enjoyed her gardens from a distance. In fact, on the most beautiful days of the summer, she and her friends played endless rounds of bridge on the sunporch. Sunshine slanted through clouds of cigarette smoke as her friends—who seemed ancient to me—barked out their bids. My mom and I both thought they were crazy to sit inside all day. Yet I happily accepted the occasional dimes or quarters that Weezie doled out from the bulging coin purse full of her earnings, which she kept "hidden" under her mattress. (My brother and I knew exactly where to find it.)

The hard work of maintaining Weezie's five acres fell to her gardener, Arthur Jones, known to us as Artie. He began to work for my grandmother just out of high school and stayed for years. Did Weezie know, when she hired him, that he had artistic talent? She may have had the initial vision for the grounds at Brook House, but Artie, whose name seemed perfect to me as a child, laid them out with an artist's eye.

Even before he came to work for my grandmother, Artie knew he wanted to paint. He studied with local artists and became known for his miniatures, as well as larger paintings of rundown barns with sagging roofs and haymows bulging with stacked bales. In his twenties, he pedaled his bike along back roads, carrying paints, rolled canvases and a palette in his bike basket as he searched for abandoned farms with a melancholy charm. During my Vermont childhood, farmers were already struggling to survive. In 1954, dairy farmers were required to purchase refrigerated bulk tanks for their milk. That ruling put an end to the sight of tin milk cans leaning against each other at the end of rutted driveways. The high cost of the tank, pipelines and automatic milking equipment marked the end for many farms. Artie's paintings attracted buyers full of nostalgia for those lost landscapes.

Artie also created soft, graceful palettes in Weezie's Brook House gardens. The gardens were shaped to fit the sloping hillside, the confluence of the brook with the river, and the view of the mountains beyond the perennial border. Clearly, Artie had a strong hand in deciding what plants went where, and he'd had some garden experience before he came to work at Brook House. In a conversation we had years after he retired from gardening, he described Weezie's M.O. "Your grandmother would be asleep when I arrived at eight sharp," Artie said. (Of course I knew this. I never ventured near her bedroom before ten, fearing the consequences.)

"Sometimes she'd raise the blind and bark at me out the window," Artie said. More often, he would decide on his own what needed to be done, and they'd consult later in the morning, when she'd finally had her second cup of hot coffee, her toast and soft-boiled eggs. Breakfast was brought upstairs to her on a bed tray, unless Grandpa Gil was home. Then, Weezie dragged herself out of bed and trudged downstairs in her diaphanous nightie, robe and blue mules. She would sit in brooding silence at one end of the curly maple table, ladling jam onto her white toast and spooning sugar into her coffee, her lips pursing in and out as if she were about to make some pronouncement.

Weezie was a tough employer, quick to criticize those who couldn't live up to her high standards. A steady stream of cooks and house cleaners came to work for her each summer. No one lasted. Some were fired after a few weeks; one quarrelsome couple quit in a fit of high temper, spewing Italian epithets; others simply wheeled out of the driveway, scattering stones, and never returned. But Artie and my grandmother got along famously, even as they fought. He wasn't afraid to stand up to her, and he refused to be treated like a servant. Even more amazing, he laughed at her rampages, rolled his eyes, and disappeared into the garden. When Artie finally quit to pursue his art full time, Weezie was bereft. The gardens suffered and she called in desperation, begging him to come back. "I miss you," she said. "We had so much fun."

"We *did?*" Artie chortled decades later, when he told me this story. My guess is that Weezie grudgingly respected Artie's artistic talent, as well as his integrity.

I tormented Artie during my Vermont summers. When Sally wasn't available and my brother was off with his friends, I followed him around while he weeded, transplanted, clipped and watered. When I was bored, or lonesome for conversation, I pestered him with questions. Artie responded with gentle teasing and tolerance. I didn't realize that I was absorbing gardening lore. If he pulled weeds on the steep stream banks beneath the footbridge, I read a book nearby. A millstone was embedded on the other side of the brook, where the bridge met the lawn. For years, I thought the stone must have been there since the houses were brought up from Enfield, until I saw his initials, AJ, etched into the cement. I was jealous that he'd found a way to memorialize himself in the gardens.

On rainy days, I followed him to the basement and watched as he arranged gladiolas. He clipped the stems and set them in the tall brown vase, seemingly without much care. Now, having seen the flower arrangements in his own house, I understand that his artist's eye was at work there, too.

Artie's personal creation was the rock garden, which he built from scratch. "It made that part of the yard more interesting," he told me years later. As he wrestled stones into place, dug out weeds and crabgrass, I only half listened. Once the garden was finished, I should have been more sympathetic to his complaints about the heat, the weeds, and the petunias. As I later learned, they needed constant de-heading.

One summer, Weezie punished me by ordering me to pick off every dead petunia blossom in Artie's rock garden. I trudged up the hill on a hot day. The faded blossoms gave off a thick, cloying fragrance, and the dead flowers stuck to my fingers as I plucked and tossed them into a bushel basket. Was this my punishment for hosting a party at Brook House while my parents were away, a party that spun wildly out of control? (Artie never said a word, though he plucked empty beer cans from under the shrubs for days and warned me, with his dry humor, that he'd spill my secret if I didn't behave.) When the work was done, I sympathized with Artie's complaints about petunias. I have never grown them since.

Artie was my first gay friend. I'd never heard the term "gay" when I was young, and I'm not sure when or how I realized that he preferred men, but it didn't matter to me. He was just Artie, my pal with the infectious laugh who understood our family dynamics and made me welcome in the garden. My father, like many straight men at the time, often dropped what I call "the other F bomb," sometimes within Artie's hearing. My mother had danced alongside gay men in Martha Graham's company and spoke fondly of her former dance colleagues, but Dad made it clear that he disapproved of Artie's "lifestyle" (as he called it).

I cringed at my father's homophobia. Now, I credit Artie both for my love of flowers, and—even more important—for the close friendships I've had with gay men and women throughout my life.

There are connoisseurs of blue
just as there are lovers of wine.
—Colette

Blue Hydrangea

Hydrangea macrophylla

A hydrangea hedge stands to the left of Weezie's perennial border, up against the stone wall. The shrubs form a barrier between the flowerbeds and the copse of pine and hemlock that overhangs the Mettawee River. Weezie's hydrangeas are not the oakleaf or lacecaps I learned to admire as an adult gardener, but the traditional shrubs with blue, ball-like blossoms. Although I love blue flowers, I have always avoided these particular hydrangeas. Their blue seems phony, almost garish; their ball shapes fake, manmade. The very name—*hydrangea*—often slips my mind.

Weezie's blue hydrangeas grow above a dank log cabin tucked under the hemlocks. This is where we change into bathing suits, before swimming in the Mettawee River. Years before my grandmother's time at Brook House, someone built concrete dams in the river, creating two waterfalls. Sometimes, when we are in the mood for adventure, my mother and I wash our hair under the first, low waterfall. A larger waterfall tumbles into a swimming hole below the second dam. On hot days, the hemlocks cast dappled shade and sunlight across the foaming water. The pool is icy cold.

The log cabin has two sections—one side for boys, the other for girls. Before swimming, Sally and I scurry into the girl's side and change as fast as we can. Spider webs make sticky tracks on our cheeks; mouse droppings and broken acorns, collected by squirrels and chipmunks, litter the floor. Sally and I hang our shorts and shirts on rusty hooks, tie the tops of our suits around our necks, and dash, barefoot, along the soft pine-needled path to the dam. We inch out onto the top of the concrete, struggling to keep our balance against the rush of current parting in V-shapes around our ankles. Our feet are numb in seconds. We squeal and shiver until one of us finally gets up the nerve to jump into the churning whirlpool below.

Relatives often visit Weezie in the summer. For two years in a row, my cousins Kezia and Eddie spend part of the summer with us. They are my mother's first cousins, though only a few years older than I am. The first year, they stay for six weeks. My mother explains that *their* mother—my great-aunt Bobby—has gone to Reno (wherever that is) to get a divorce from her husband Edwin. I have no idea how this works, or why anyone would go so far to end a marriage. I have met my cousins' father a few times; he was elegant and good-looking, with a twinkle in his eye. Why would Bobby leave him?

I *do* know that we are not supposed to mention the divorce. It is, as Great-aunt Bobby would say, "graveyard:" her term for a secret that stays within the family. There are many levels of "graveyard," from Double, Triple, and—the most serious—Quadruple. Bobby's divorce from Edwin is Quadruple Graveyard.

Kezia, my older cousin, is tall and big-boned, with long black hair and dazzling blue eyes. And she's dramatic. Her temper tantrums shake our little house as she slams doors, shivers the glass and yells at everyone. Five minutes later, she will be organizing the kids in our neighborhood into a play, which she writes and directs, while taking the starring role. It is no surprise to any of us that Kezia later becomes a model, works for Vogue, marries three (or is it four?) times—including to two gay men who once were business partners as well as lovers. The three of them end up living in the same Manhattan apartment building with their daughter, where they direct dazzling fashion shoots.

Eddie, Kezia's younger brother, is sullen and quiet that first summer. The following year, the cousins return with Peter Mott, their new stepbrother. Eddie and Peter set out to make my life hell—or at least that's how it feels to me. (Looking back, I imagine they were each living in misery: two awkward preteens with their families torn apart, then mashed together into a stew of strangers.) My mother tries to enlist me as a sympathetic ally. "They're going through a tough time," she says. "Try to understand."

(Sure Mom.)

One afternoon, I hurry past the hydrangea border, slip into the log cabin above the river and pull off my clothes. As I try to wrestle my cold, damp suit up over my skinny legs and butt, I hear whistles and jeers. Eddie and Peter hoot at me from the other side of the wall. I freeze. A long finger pokes through a knothole. It wiggles obscenely, like a skinless snake.

I cross my arms over my naked chest, though there is nothing to hide. I stumble and trip as I toss my suit aside, pull on my clothes and dash from the building, my shorts twisted at my waist. I stub my toe on a hemlock root but keep going, dodging the hydrangea hedge. Eddie and Peter jog after me. Their catcalls sting like slaps. Their voices break, on a slip-slide between bass and soprano. I don't remember specific words, just the venomous taunts and my shame. They've seen me, flat-chested and shapeless, my crooked spine that inspires the class bully to call me "hunchback."

I hate blue hydrangeas.

Such geraniums!
It does not become us poor mortals to be vain but really, my geraniums!
—Mary Mitford
Our Village

Geranium

Pelargonium peltatum

In the summer months, Weezie's cocktail hour takes place on the slate terrace, on the south side of the house. The charcoal gray slate comes from the nearby quarries of West Pawlet and Granville. Wrought-iron railings separate the terrace from the lawn and driveway below. The terrace also marks the formal entrance to the official front door—but, as in most Vermont houses, we usually go in and out through the kitchen.

Weezie holds the place of honor: the pink-cushioned, metal love seat with the best view of the mountains. She sits with her legs crossed, one ankle flexed to show off her legs. As she raises and lowers the top leg, admiring it, Grandpa Gil catches my eye and winks. (We know that Weezie considers her legs her best feature.) Ice clinks in Weezie's glass as she sips her amber scotch. "Just half an ounce, with plenty of ice," she tells my dad as she thrusts out her glass for a second drink—as if Dad hasn't been making her drinks for years.

The cushions on Weezie's porch furniture match the bright pink geraniums that bob in the window boxes, as well as the garish fuchsia-pink pool furniture at the foot of her yard. Each spring, after the last frost, Artie Jones fills the terrace planters with potting soil and geraniums, tending them through the summer and then repotting them in clay pots in the fall. They bloom on Weezie's sunporch throughout the winter. For me, as a child, the geraniums are background.

If Weezie has guests from her social group—her bridge partners and their husbands, or neighbors who seem ancient to me—my appearance is a command performance. I make the rounds, shake hands politely, then perch on the edge of a chair or balance on the wrought iron railing, waiting to be released so I can return to my book. If only I could escape, like my brother Tom and his friends! Heads shaved in identical summer crew cuts, the boys race up and down the driveway on their bikes, or play under a maple tree with the elaborate miniature farm that they've created in a sand pile. Why are they free, while I'm trapped here?

The view from the terrace seems arranged in steps: first, the stone wall that runs along the driveway; then the white bridge crossing the stream that leads to the perennial gardens beyond. The gardens themselves border another stone wall that marks the boundary between Weezie's property and the Hart farm's hayfield beyond. The mountain we call The Saddle—because of its shape—is a majestic presence in the distance.

The Saddle meadows are mowed once every summer, so the Saddle's seat and its pommel are a lighter green than the darker woods below. When our Harwell or Grayson aunts, uncles and cousins come to visit, we hike to the Saddle's high fields, carrying a picnic lunch. My father has seen an eagle there (a rare sighting, during the days of DDT). Years later, I will spot a bear eating blackberries at the field's highest point. Though I never tell anyone, I have already decided that someday I will be married with that spectacular view as a backdrop.

If the sun shines, family gatherings also take place on the terrace. When Weezie's sisters visit, as they often do in the summer, their friendly bickering dominates the conversation. Catfights break out as quickly as laughter. Weezie is the eldest by many years. She and her next two siblings—a girl, Helen, and a brother, Jonathan—all came down with typhoid fever in childhood. Only Weezie survived, though her hair fell out and she was sickly for a long time. Years later, two younger sisters—my great-aunts Bobby and Jane (called Dee)—were born. Just a few years older than my mother, they are more like Mom's older sisters than her aunts.

(At the end of her life, Weezie tells me, in secret, that the spirit of her lost sister Helen sometimes appeared to her—including once, at a dinner party, when a stranger sitting next to her said, quietly, "There's a child standing behind you. Her name starts with an H—*Helen* perhaps?" I found this story spooky, but Weezie was comforted to know that her sister was still with her. And I was flattered that Weezie shared her spiritual side with me—an aspect of her personality that rarely emerged in family gatherings.)

When Bobby and Dee visit, the atmosphere is electric. Doors slam and heels trip-trap on the wood floors as childhood rivalries and fierce jealousies erupt. Inside the house, the aunts argue over their matching black patent leather, quilted pocketbooks with gold chains. "I bought mine before you did," Aunt Bobby insists. The youngest by far, Bobby still has to prove she's not a copycat.

I believe her about the purse. After all, Bobby is a skilled shopper, an interior designer with an inside track—and steep discounts—in the Garment District, on New York's Seventh Avenue. Bobby sometimes takes me there, where I marvel at workers wheeling racks of mink coats or ball gowns through city traffic.

The aunts' husbands, George and Rob, exchange amused glances or gravitate toward my dad when arguments escalate. But the sisters don't fight on the terrace. Perhaps because the grown-ups have changed for dinner, or maybe thanks to the lubrication of alcohol, the cocktail hour inspires laughter, easy chatter and story-telling. When our Nashville cousins visit, they bring their guitars and we all sing. The geraniums add color in the background.

Years later, these geraniums are in bloom when my father and I cross Weezie's terrace on my first wedding day—just as I had once imagined. A black-and-white photo of that moment captures the mask of terror that immobilized my dad's face before he opened the door, took my arm, and led me across the bridge and up the slate path to the garden. Perhaps he was trying not to weep as he gave his daughter away. Or maybe he worried that I was too young to fly into a new life—though he was just twenty-one himself when he married my mother, in a marriage that lasted almost seventy years.

Brook House was sold a few years after my wedding. By then, Weezie's health had declined and she bought a small house in the village. My parents built a new house on the hill above their barn, and my mother potted up some of the geraniums. The flowers thrived in the warm, south-facing windows of the dining room. When my husband Casey and I built our home in Marlboro, Vermont, my mother gave me cuttings from those originals. Weezie's geraniums bloomed in our chilly dining room in the winter, and on our front porch in the summers. They flowered reliably as our sons were born, grew up and left home for college and adult life.

When my marriage ended, two pots of these geraniums kept me company as I struggled to make a new life in another Vermont town, then in Massachusetts.

Now they bloom on a south-facing balcony outside our city home. On the other side of Boston, a descendant of Weezie's plants flourishes in my younger son Ethan's house. (He and his wife, Vita, do well with houseplants.) The geraniums match the generations: mine is the granddaughter of Weezie's original plants; Ethan's plant is its healthy great-grandchild.

Finally, I gave a few cuttings to Artie Jones, who had cared for Weezie's original plants through many Vermont winters. In his nineties, Artie still had a green thumb. He called a few months after the transplants were settled. "Your geranium is blooming!" he announced. When I visited, he steered me to the geranium right away, proud of its vigorous blooms.

I write this on an October day with frost in the forecast. I have just brought my geraniums inside for the winter. I give them bigger pots with fresh soil and breathe in their musky smell. One whiff and I'm on the terrace again. Weezie's ice clinks in her glass. My father leans against the railing, cigarette in hand, his eyes on the Saddle, which he dreams of owning someday. (And he will.) My mother is on the move as always, darting into the house for a plate of cheese and crackers or to check on dinner. Everyone in those generations is gone, but the flowers bring my family back.

Plant a carrot, get a carrot
Not a brussel sprout
That's why I like vegetables
You know what you're about!
Life is merry,
If it's very
Vegetarian!
—The Fantasticks

Shining Willow

Salix lucida

At Brook House, my mother's vegetable garden was near the guest house, spread out beside a willow tree. This was not the ubiquitous, weeping willow, but an upright tree with glossy leaves that flipped over in wind or rainstorms, shifting from dark green to quicksilver. Like my mother, the professional dancer, this willow was tall and straight. A search through a list of willow varieties brings up a picture of *salix lucida* that matches my memory of the tree, which produced soft white catkins in the spring. Like other willows, it was happy growing beside the stream, where its feet stayed wet.

While I later learned about gardening from Artie Jones by osmosis, trailing him around and watching him work, my mother was my first true garden teacher. I have no idea where or when *she* learned to garden. Was it on her grandparents' farm, outside of Youngstown, Ohio? Having seen pictures of the formal stone house her parents built in Sewickley, Pennsylvania, it's hard to imagine they grew vegetables there. Did she learn from our Vermont neighbors? She gardened as if it came naturally. I never thought to ask her how she learned—and now it's too late. I can only recreate, in my mind, the little garden we worked in together, more than sixty years ago.

I was probably not much help in that garden. When I was six or seven, Mom decided I was old enough to weed the dreaded beets (I hated their taste then). Though Mom showed me the difference between the shiny red-green leaves of the beets and the weeds poking through black soil, I probably yanked out many tiny beets by mistake. Thinning Bibb lettuce was another tough chore for a child with clumsy fingers. I remember the rich smell of fertile soil, the delicate green of lacy carrot tops contrasting with dark earth, the miracle of sturdy bean leaves that unfolded overnight from a curled embryo. There must have been stones and mosquitoes, seeds that never germinated, and marauders such as rabbits and woodchucks—but what I recall most about that garden is that Mom and I were content there.

My mother sang while we hoed and pulled weeds. Earthworms wiggled and twisted as we exposed them to the sun. My knees were caked with dirt; my arms covered with bloody smudges where I'd slapped at horse flies. The sun was hot on my back. I longed to stop and dangle my bare feet in the icy current of the brook nearby. Mom promised we'd swim when the weeding was done.

Like the willow leaves in a burst of summer rain, my mother's mood could flip without warning. One moment, she was the tolerant, creative woman who organized a pet show (with my dad) in the driveway below the guest house. Every child who brought a pet received a blue ribbon. The animals ranged from a tiny frog in a shoebox to a horse whose mahogany coat shone from repeated brushings. My mother adored animals and couldn't bear to see them suffer. I once listened in fear as she sobbed in the bathtub, behind a locked door, after she had driven over a child's new kitten.

Although she was a neatnik, Mom tolerated the elaborate games that Tom and I set up with our stuffed animals, as we moved the living room furniture to create castles, stores and Tom's favorite battle scenes. When our cousin Kezia visited, the summer of her family's divorce, Mom helped her string a curtain across one end of the living room and invited the neighborhood kids to participate in the plays that Kezia wrote and directed.

The flip side was Mom's sudden bursts of temper, which were unpredictable. Her eyes flashed, her dancer's body, a coil of energy, seemed poised to strike—though she rarely did. (I remember, as if my cheek still burns, the one time she slapped my face. I was a rude teen, hurtling down the dark back stairs at Brook House. I don't recall what I said, just that I had sassed her one too many times. I tried to push past but she slapped me—hard—shocking us both.) When she was angry, her words also stung. I shrank into my shell and ran for the safety of the wooden platform in the cherry tree, where I read and reread my favorite novels for comfort.

We had one summer of constant rain—at least, that's how I remember it. Did we even have a garden that year? Rain beat against the windows and weighed the branches of the pines outside the living room window of the guesthouse. I lay in my downstairs bedroom at night with the windows shut against the roar of the brook; the rumble and clacking of stones in the Mettawee River.

Was that the summer my mother jacked up the radio whenever "The Wayward Wind" came on the radio? She sang along at top volume herself, whipping from one room to another in our small house like a tiger in a cage, brown eyes flashing, jean skirt slapping at her knees. I worried. Did she also "yearn to wander" like the singer who was born "next of kin" to that wind? Dad only came up from the city on weekends. If Mom disappeared, would we be left alone with the rain?

Perhaps that was why I weeded and thinned beside her without complaint. When we worked in the garden, she seemed anchored to the wet soil, the feathery carrot tops, and the hoe in her hands. We hummed and the leaves of the willow shimmered in the breeze. Mom was genuinely happy in that garden.

There was every joy on earth in the secret garden that morning, and in the midst of them came a delight more delightful than all...
—Frances Hodgson Burnett
The Secret Garden

English Ivy

Hedera helix

Did reading *The Secret Garden* turn me into a gardener? Or was I already drawn to gardens and thus found myself in its pages? What caused me to read the novel over and over? Was it the thrill that Mary felt when the robin showed her the key, the shiver that ran down my spine when a breeze lifted the tangle of ivy and revealed the lock? Was it the feeling of ownership that Mary discovered when she stepped into that walled Eden? Or was I drawn to the way that Mary—a spoiled, lonely, crabby orphan—came to life herself, along with the garden in spring? I was probably Mary's age when I first read the novel. (Of course *I* was never as selfish or as ornery as Mary—was I?)

I loved Dickon and adored the lilting pattern of his Yorkshire dialect. "'We munnot stir,' Dickon whispered. 'We munnot scarce breathe.'" And like Mary when Dickon spoke, I could scarcely breathe myself. I didn't mind the misspellings (which would be frowned on today); instead, I enjoyed the puzzle of sounding out his language and hearing it in my head. I envied Dickon, his pet fox and the crow that sat on his shoulder. I longed to see the purpling moor, the "strange grey mist" that Mary witnessed as the roses came to life.

My copy of the novel was already well worn the first time I read it. Had it been my mother's? I entered the world of that garden, set on the Yorkshire moor, while sitting on the small, triangular platform that my father had built in the forked branches of a cherry tree. Too small to be called a tree house, my reading hideout overlooked the Mettawee River. My perch was rudimentary, compared to our neighbor Malcy's elaborate tree house across the road. Perched high in a white pine, Malcy's aerie boasted furniture, windows, pulleys, and a slick pole—which Mom once shimmied up, agile as ever, shocking Malc. (He wished he'd had time to hide his girly magazines, but Mom, to his delight, never gave him away.)

In contrast, my simple platform was in an isolated spot near the tool shed. Even Artie rarely passed by, unless he needed a shovel or something larger than his small hand tools. I read facing the hemlocks that leaned over the river, my feet dangling above the riverbank. The Mettawee's rush was soothing background noise.

Never mind that Brook House already boasted perennial borders and lovely shade gardens sloping to the stream—I wanted my own secret garden with an iron key that turned in a rusty, hidden lock; rose bushes that climbed walls of warm stone; and a friend like Dickon who had a way with injured children as well as wild animals. Though I knew the ending, I read the novel over and over again. I was thrilled by Colin's transformation from a sickly, spoiled "rajah" to a healthy boy who could run and laugh and dig in the warm spring earth. Though I couldn't have named the story's power when I was young, *The Secret Garden* taught me that gardens can heal the body—and the mind. Now, I sometimes wonder if I have been trying—all my life—to recreate that fictional garden, every time I have built a garden from scratch.

Part Two
Shaping the Landscape: Learning from the Elders

We are all just walking each other home.
—Ram Dass

There is a special period, the little-understood, prepubertal, halcyon,
middle age of childhood...when the natural world
is experienced in some highly evocative way...
—Edith Cobb
The Ecology of Imagination in Childhood

Beets

Beta vulgaris

The summer I turned twelve, I
left home to spend eight weeks at Treetops, a progressive camp in the
High Peaks of the Adirondacks. That first year, I lived with three other
girls in a canvas tent overlooking Round Lake. At dawn, mist skimmed
the lake's dark surface like strands of fleece pulled thin by carding.
When we rolled up the canvas on the sides of our tent, we looked out at
Balanced Rocks and Cascade Mountain, two peaks I would climb often. At
night, a loon's lonesome, eerie cry sometimes woke me from sleep. We
had no electricity in our living spaces; no telephone or access to radio or

television. My mother and grandmother wept when they dropped me off for the first time. What was *wrong* with them? Couldn't they see this was paradise?

Though I didn't realize it at the time, my six summers at Treetops—three as a camper, another three as a counselor—would shape my political outlook, my feelings about the environment and gardening, my theories of education, and my involvement in social action. My work as a counselor taught me more about learning and child development than any education class I took in grad school.

The camp also opened my eyes to a wider world than the exclusive suburb where I spent my school years. At that time, Bronxville, New York was a town with restrictive racist and anti-Semitic real estate covenants. (Covenants that, I was appalled to learn, were upheld by my great-uncle George, a realtor.) Treetops was one of the first biracial camps in the country and, thanks to a strong scholarship program and a wide outreach, it attracted children from a variety of backgrounds. My concern for social justice and racial equality were nourished there. I played music with counselors who had fled Nazi Germany; lived with Jewish tentmates and made friends with campers from other countries, as well as Black children from New York and other cities. Many—returning as counselors the way I did—became lifelong friends, including Reg Gilliam, who grew up in Harlem's Sugar Hill neighborhood, earned a Harvard Law degree, worked on Capitol Hill and was appointed to the Interstate Commerce Commission under President Carter. Nothing that I learned in formal school would come close to the education I received at Treetops.

I also grew physically stronger there. A skinny, sickly child (due, perhaps, to living with second-hand smoke at home), I gained strength and skills as we climbed Adirondack peaks, canoed in lakes and remote rivers, and bivouacked in scrubby alpine forests. I sailed and rowed, and in my final summer as a camper, passed Junior Red Cross Life Saving. And everyone gardened.

Treetops was where I first heard the term "organic gardening." The camp was ahead of its time in its awareness of the dangers of pesticides.

When New York State promoted the aerial spraying of DDT in the fifties, the camp and North Country School—which shared the same property—tied giant balloons to their tallest spruce trees to mark the property's boundaries and warn the planes away from their forests and gardens.

At Treetops, we each had responsibility for specific rows in the large vegetable garden. Those vegetables fed us campers, as well as the boarding students who spent the school years at North Country School. Thanks to the gardening I had done with my mother, I understood the connection between the food we grew and what we ate—at least in the summer. As a toddler, I had slipped my hands under the hens in our chicken house, to pull out their freshly laid eggs. Later, I caught bass and trout at my godfather's Adirondack camp, then learned how to clean and cook the fish. But until I went to Treetops, I had never plucked a chicken that I would eat. This was a gritty, smelly job that campers and staff did together, working in shifts on a hot summer day. Though I'd grown up near dairy farms, I'd never milked a cow—which I soon learned to do—or fed piglets, animals that impressed me with their intelligence, yet provided bacon for breakfast the following summer.

This learning took place under the guidance of the camp director, Helen Haskell. A visionary and progressive in the field of education, Helen led by example and inspiration. She believed that "unless you give something to an institution, you don't really belong to it." With this in mind, campers signed up for weekly jobs that included caring for a favorite animal in the barn; setting tables; cleaning kerosene lanterns and trimming their wicks; arranging flowers; chopping and stacking wood. We also had group chores related to the garden. We gathered before lunch to sing as we shelled bushels of peas or snapped beans for dinner. An outbreak of potato bugs brought everyone to the potato patch to pick off the sticky bugs and drop them into kerosene: a nasty job. On the other hand, when strawberries were ripe, no one minded the call to harvest juicy berries for shortcake.

Like Helen Haskell, I was an early riser, and I enjoyed barn chores. Though a nervous rider, I loved the smell of the horses, the scent of hay, the stickiness of oats on my skin as I poured grain into a feed trough, the contented snuffling of the horses as they were fed, the ripple of their skin under the curry comb, the tickle of their whiskers against my wrist as I buckled a halter. The barn had an enormous hayloft. Standing inside the wide barn doors, watching barn swallows wheel from sunshine to shade, I felt I had entered the magical barn that E.B. White brought to life in *Charlotte's Web*.

On the days when I had barn chores, a counselor woke me with a whisper, or a light tap on the shoulder. I slipped into my damp barn clothes, still smelling horsey from the day before, and joined my fellow campers on the long walk to the barn. Too sleepy to talk, we rubbed our eyes and drew fingers through our tangled hair as we stumbled down the dirt road.

If the weather was fine, Helen was already at work in the flowerbed that ran along one side of the driveway. A slight, wiry woman, her prematurely white hair tied back with a red bandanna, Helen sometimes waved to us—but often, bent over with clippers or trowel in hand, she seemed oblivious to our passing. (Helen was actually quite deaf. I wonder now if she kept her hearing aids turned off on those mornings, to give herself an hour of peace before the hubbub of breakfast.)

Helen's flowerbeds were filled with annuals. When I returned to camp as a counselor, I knew the flowers by their names—zinnias, marigolds, snapdragons—but as a child, I barely paid attention. I noticed their bright colors—red, orange, yellow, pink, white—set against the green of the hayfield beyond the split rail fence, but I took the flowerbeds for granted. On a recent visit, fifty years after my childhood summers, I realized that the driveway was, in fact, as long as I remembered—and that tending those flowerbeds had always been a huge job.

I enjoyed taking care of a horse for a week. Sugar, a speckled gray pony, was my favorite, even though she once stepped in a nest of ground bees and threw me into a thicket of weeds. I stood up laughing. But I dreaded the work in the vegetable garden. Each tent or lean-to group was assigned specific rows to tend for the summer. For some reason, my group always ended up with beets. My tentmates and I grumbled as we weeded, cultivated and thinned the plants, which were tiny and delicate when summer began. In a repeat of my experience in my mom's Dorset garden, I probably pulled out as many beet seedlings as weeds. Mosquitoes and horse flies loved our shady end of the garden near the woods. We slapped our shoulders and rubbed our necks until our skin was caked with wet dirt. Why did the older campers—assigned to sweet corn or strawberries—get the best deals?

When I returned to camp as a counselor, I volunteered for a new assignment. On Sunday evenings, I was in charge of shaping the compost—a polite name for the manure pile at the back of the barn. Dressed in knee-high boots and rank jeans that could almost stand on their own, I stood below the open door and waited for the "honey wagon" to arrive: a malodorous, manure-encrusted cart, suspended by chains from a track that ran along the ceiling. Two older campers pulled the honey wagon through the barn, stopping behind each horse stall to shovel in the fresh manure. Eventually, full and steaming, the cart careened out the door to the end of the track. The rattle of gears and the shouts of children warned me to hold my breath and jump out of the way as the load tipped out. It was my job—aided by a couple of strong kids who got a similar, weird charge out of this work—to shape the pile.

In contrast to Helen's sweet-smelling flowerbeds, the manure pile was odorous and mucky. But Helen and her brother, Walter Clark, knew that this rank pile, properly turned and shaped, would eventually become rich, healthy soil. Camp meals created buckets of food scraps; whatever the pigs wouldn't eat was trucked in an old Jeep to the pile. My child helpers and I forked the food garbage into the hot manure, turning and smoothing the stinky mess—a pile ten to twelve feet long—until it took on the shape of a loaf of bread that had collapsed in the middle. Later in the summer, Walter would move the pile to a field close to the garden for further ripening. Eventually it became rich soil, feeding the plants that ended up on our dinner table.

This cycle is well known to anyone who is serious about gardening. Ten years later, living on a small farm in Vermont where my first husband and I raised vegetables, a small flock of sheep, and a few goats, I found myself shaping a much smaller manure pile. Swallows flew overhead, snatching at flies, and I recalled Helen Haskell's thin, reedy voice, full of passion as she talked to us about the natural world and our role as caretakers of the environment. As children, we snickered when she extolled nature in almost spiritual terms. Such deep emotion made us jittery.

Later, as young adult counselors, we rolled our eyes when she spoke of children, plants, and mountains with the same reverence. Now I realize that Helen approached people and plants in the same way. She taught us that every living thing needs clean water, sunshine, good food, love and encouragement. She respected our individual differences, yet taught us to work on behalf of the larger community. And somehow, she made us feel that, if we set our minds to it, we too could flower, creating beauty as she did when she tended her flowers beside the dusty road.

This morning the green fists of the peonies
are getting ready to break my heart as the sun rises,
as the sun strokes them with his old, buttery fingers...
—Mary Oliver
Peonies

Peony

Paeonia lactiflora "Alba"

A garden can never have too many peonies or foxgloves. This is my own first rule of gardening. I adore peonies. I admire their upright stance and glossy foliage, attractive long after the flowers scatter their faded petals. The blossoms of double peonies remind me of pretty summer frocks, pastel layers of tulle and organza, while a single peony is more delicate, like a girl who wears her heart on her sleeve. Until climate change altered bloom dates, my own peonies often opened on or near my birthday in June—but my love for them is deeper than any date on the calendar.

I'm also fascinated by the relationship of peonies and ants. Like many gardeners, I once assumed that the arrival of ants, when peony buds are forming, was necessary for the buds to open. I learned later that the glands on the buds produce nectar composed of sugar, amino acids, and water: a heavenly ambrosia for ants. The ants, in turn, keep other pests away. Though the buds would open without the ants, it's a symbiotic relationship.

When I first became aware of peonies, I wasn't interested in the science of plants. My father's mother, Pat Ketchum (whom we called "Frustie," for some unknown reason), was an avid gardener, blessed with the greenest thumb in the family. Her peonies were stunning.

The oldest of five grandchildren, I was born to young parents whose parents also had children early, so I was lucky to know three of my grandparents into my own adulthood. Frustie lived the longest, dying when I was in my late forties. We had a complicated relationship. She played favorites (preferring girls over boys, which offended me on my brother's behalf, as well as my boy cousins). Worse, she was nasty to my mother, blaming her for my father's decision not to join my grandfather's advertising business—although my parents made that decision together. Frustie was small-minded, racist, and virulently anti-Semitic. Her nasty slurs made me squirm.

Still, I admired her energy and her many talents. No matter what she did, Frustie's hands moved in a blur that made me feel even clumsier than usual. She stitched and smocked dresses for my cousin Katherine and me, and made the world's best fudge frosting (while keeping the exact recipe a secret). She weeded, transplanted and clipped in her flower gardens, which won awards—as did her floral arrangements. An amateur painter, Frustie began sculpting in her fifties, creating graceful sculptures for the fountains at their Florida home.

My earliest memories of Frustie come from the years when my grandparents still lived full time in Pittsburgh. When I was seven or eight, I traveled from Washington, D.C. to spend a week alone with them. I stayed in the house they had built on Linden Avenue, in Pittsburgh's

Squirrel Hill district, where my dad and my aunt grew up. It must have had a nice yard, but my memories of that visit are hazy. I can picture the canopy bed I slept in (where I had nightmares) and the dank basement where I tried, in vain, to enjoy playing with my aunt's dollhouse—a structure so grand that it took up most of a Ping-Pong table. For the first time in my life, I was desperately homesick. Finally, my grandfather— whom I adored—stormed into the guest room in frustration. "I'll take you home tomorrow," he barked, "if you'll just stop that damned crying!"

Grandpa had never raised his voice at me. I was shocked into silence. The next morning, as promised, he and I rode the sleeper back to Washington, D.C. My grandfather turned around and took the next train home. Now all that I know about the Linden Avenue gardens comes from family stories. That generation is gone.

During the Depression years, Frustie told me, she grew all their vegetables in their backyard. Grandpa managed to keep his advertising agency going without laying anyone off—a miracle in that era. (Decades later, when my dad unearthed Grandpa's tax returns from the 1930s, he saw that his father often didn't take a salary during those years.) Frustie's vegetable garden filled the family's larder and fed the destitute men who knocked at their back door, hoping for a handout. Her generosity to those homeless men surprised me when I learned about it later. Perhaps she remembered the hardships of her own childhood. Frustie also boasted that her Second World War Victory Garden was even bigger than her Depression-era plot.

A few years after my first—disastrous—childhood visit, my grandparents moved from downtown Pittsburgh to suburban Fox Chapel. I remember that property and its gardens as magical. In Washington, D.C., where we lived at the time, my family was uprooted constantly, shifting from one rental to another. We stayed in houses with non-descript yards, so my grandparents' yard in Fox Chapel seemed lush and spacious. My cousin Katherine remembers "acres of roses," nourished with rich, composted horse manure that mushroom growers had turned into dark soil.

On my visits, I was most intrigued by the back yard, which sloped away from the more formal gardens. It ended in a tangle of brush and woods that was deliciously scary. A muddy stream trickled in the shadows of the underbrush. Bent and twisted branches became, in my games, the roofs and walls of forts or houses. The yard also boasted cutting gardens full of flowers whose fragrance—when Frustie arranged them in vases— mingled with the scent of chopped nuts and sweet buttery cookies baked by Adelaide, their strict vegetarian cook. (As an adult, I squirmed, wondering how Adelaide felt about having to prepare and serve meat to my grandparents every day.)

And at Fox Chapel, there were peonies. I remember masses of bloom, so I must have visited in June. Frustie and I both had June birthdays. Perhaps this accounted for our joint love of these flowers. Sadly, we couldn't connect in other ways. We were like oil and water, politically as well as personally, so I sometimes tuned her out when I might have learned more about trees, shrubs and perennials.

In contrast to Weezie, who rarely got her hands dirty, Frustie worked hard in her flowerbeds. She gardened in dresses, most often a faded pink linen shift, monogrammed with her initials—TPK—in a looping script. Her hand clippers and small weeding tools seemed incongruous next to her manicured nails. Whether cultivating, picking fruit and vegetables, or cutting flowers, Frustie tripped around the yard in a matching pair of worn, pink pumps. They no longer had arch support and the heels were worn to stubs, yet she wore them until she was confined to a wheelchair. (We joked that she should be buried in those pink pumps, but Frustie was adamant: "Dress me in my best ball gown," she said. She got her wish and went out, after she died, in the silver-gray silk dress that had swished when she twirled on the dance floor. She also wore its matching shoes.)

When I was creating my first garden in Vermont, Frustie sent me a half-dozen peony plants from her favorite nursery. Our soil was thin, stony and acid. I was nervous as I followed the instructions, so I gave the plants a good dose of compost and set the plants' "eyes"—those small, hopeful nubs—facing upward. When the peonies bloomed, a few years later, they revealed the varieties I remembered from Frustie's garden, including my favorite, the lush *festiva maxima*.

Nothing moved Frustie as much as a plant (or a dog) in distress. Every plant had its use, whether as an ornament for the house or food for the table, so they all deserved equal attention. A few years after we had created our first vegetable and flower gardens, Frustie arrived for a visit. A dramatic thunderstorm whipped in from the northwest. She stood at our picture window, watching as lightning streaked the sky. Thunder rolled and suddenly, the warm drumming of rain switched to the staccato ping of hail. We watched, helpless, as icy stones lashed the young corn plants in our vegetable garden and tore the petals from my roses.

When the storm was over, cornstalks lay on the ground, battered and limp. Frustie borrowed my sneakers and an old raincoat and clomped out into the soggy rows, my coat dragging on the ground behind her. She gathered stones in her skirt and propped up each stalk with painstaking care, using the rocks to hold them in place. The corn recovered and we had a fine crop in August.

On another summer visit, Frustie grew restless. I found her at a side window in the living room. She looked longingly at the brushy, unkempt area beneath the power line, overgrown with goldenrod, hardhack and ferns. "Could I borrow your clippers?" she asked.

She tripped outside, wearing the inevitable pink shoes, and returned an hour later, flushed and happy. Her stockings were torn and flecked with burrs, her arms full of ordinary grasses and weeds. She scrounged the kitchen cabinets for tall Mason jars and soon created arrangements that featured native grasses and ferns, as well as potentilla that had been hidden in the brush. These arrangements could have won prizes from an Ikebana master. She made beauty where I saw a tangle of weeds.

On each Vermont visit, Frustie admired our peonies, whether they were in bloom, or showing off their glossy foliage against the granite retaining wall. When my first marriage ended, I dug up six of her plants, transplanting them twice before giving them a permanent home in our city garden. They struggled the first year or two and then—a few years later—they bloomed profusely, but changed color from pink to white. Were they reminding me that peonies hate to be moved?

Frustie passed her love of peonies on to other family members. When my dad was still alive, the pink and maroon peonies that she gave him bloomed against the wall of his Vermont writing studio. My aunt Janet grew peonies, also a gift from Frustie, on their farm in Virginia. Now Janet has also departed for a more heavenly garden. After my parents died, twelve weeks apart, it seemed appropriate to plant peonies on either side of their headstone. Each boasted a single golden blossom the first year. According to the *Encyclopedia of Organic Gardening*, peonies can live happily for forty years or more. In this way, they share my grandmother's positive traits: tough, enduring, and showy.

I learned to respect the garden, where rituals and right actions prevailed.
Patience was requisite.
There was redemption in silence. Seasons were restorative.
A garden, I realized, heals.
—Anthony Shadid
House of Stone

Bottlebrush Tree

Callistemon rigidus

Now that I've gardened in a few different climates, I realize that my grandparents' Florida gardens were a triumph. In spite of sandy soil, slugs and other pests, sudden cloudbursts and rampant weeds, Frustie managed to grow tasty vegetables, grapefruit for our breakfasts, lemons and limes, and plants I'd never seen.

When my sons were young, we often visited in March, during Vermont's grueling mud season. One afternoon, I followed Frustie into the sandy yard behind the kitchen of her house. Dressed in her ubiquitous pink pumps, she took me into the walled back yard and pointed to a tree with sparse leaves and flowers shaped like a bottlebrush. "Look at those flowers," she said, and waved her clippers at the upright, brushy pink flowers standing at the end of long bare stalks. "Just like its name."

I was gardening myself then, learning on the fly, with a growing interest in plants from different regions, with varying needs. Perhaps I'd seen this tree before; if so, I'd forgotten. It was odd—not shapely or elegant—but I knew that Frustie would find a way to arrange those flowers into an appealing design.

My grandparents' second home in Florida sat on a bluff overlooking the ocean. Neighboring houses were owned by wealthy C.E.O.s and their well-dressed, well-coiffed, manicured wives. Some owned companies represented by my grandfather's Pittsburgh ad agency. Frustie liked dropping their names as well as their brands (Alcoa, Heinz, Westinghouse, Johnson & Johnson.) She wasn't keen on mentioning the man who headed Kohler toilets—a pun my father enjoyed—though she certainly knew him.

Yet while the women on the island golfed, played tennis or spent time at the spa during daytime hours, Frustie was in the garden cutting snapdragons for her next arrangement. Was she aware—even ashamed—of the vast distance between her simpler upbringing and this life of privilege?

She was born Thelma June Patten, the daughter of vaudeville parents whose elopement was a scandal. According to my father, Frustie's mother—a talented pianist and singer—slipped away in the middle of the night with her red-headed sweetheart, a fiddler on vaudeville stages. She left her beloved canary behind. In the morning, her parents discovered their daughter's empty bed and the canary lying dead in its cage—a dark omen. (I couldn't resist using this story years later, in my novel about a girl who runs away from home to sing on vaudeville stages.)

Frustie's parents divorced—a second scandal in those days—and Frustie, her younger brother and their mother returned to the little town of Shreve, Ohio. Were Frustie and her brother born on the road? Did she ever see her parents perform? I longed to hear stories of her childhood before the divorce, but Frustie's mouth set in a straight line, and her hands became busy, arranging flowers or mending a torn blouse, when I asked about her parents. "My father rarely came to visit," she told me once, out of the blue. "When he did, he always took us out for ice cream. I've hated ice cream ever since."

Though Frustie was ashamed of her parents, she had inherited their musical talents. And she obviously yearned for her missing father. After each of my sons was born, she asked: "Does he have red hair?" (Neither one did.)

Frustie and her brother were the youngest members of four generations that shared a small house in Shreve. After her divorce, Frustie's mother gave piano lessons and took in sewing to support her children. Frustie's grandfather—the only adult male in the house—ran the local hardware store. All the women were strong-willed, especially the great-grandmother, who smoked a pipe and once shoved it into her pocket when the minister came to visit, setting her skirt on fire. She also had nightly "sinking spells" that only a glass of sherry (in a teetotalers' home) could "cure."

When my younger son Ethan and I visited colleges in Ohio, we took a detour and drove to Shreve. It was still a small community, set in the heart of Amish farm country. Cresting the hills outside town, we swerved to avoid buggies pulled by glossy, high-stepping horses. During my childhood, my father, as well as Frustie, always raved about the enormous vegetable garden in Shreve, where the family had raised their food. Frustie told me about the hours she spent stirring apple butter in a big pot with a wooden paddle, to keep it from scorching. She described the cherry pitting tool (presumably from her grandfather's hardware store) and the jars of fruit, pickles and canned vegetables the family put aside for winter.

Frustie's home was long gone from the family, but Ethan and I found her house easily; the street names hadn't changed. The house—and the town—had seen better days. Rusted trailers sat on weedy cement platforms in the lot where Frustie's family once raised their fruit trees and vegetables. An abandoned oil well loomed in her former back yard like a prop left over from a film set, its pump end raised to the sky. The main street looked shabby and neglected. There was no sign of the hardware store.

It's impossible to write about my grandparents without thinking of the privileged world they lived in, as adults—in contrast to the hardships they encountered as children and adolescents. Frustie went to work as a secretary straight out of high school. Did she feel lost later in life, among my grandfather's wealthy clients? Did that insecurity cause her to disparage those who were struggling or hadn't advanced as she had?

For as long as I knew her, Frustie criticized the cooks and maids who worked in her steamy kitchen over the years, as well as the yard man who cut the grass and picked up fallen palm branches. Millie Mickens, the talented Black cook who worked for my parents in the summer and (reluctantly) for Frustie for a few winters, complained to me bitterly about my grandmother's racist remarks, filling me with shame. I often made friends with the staff (which made Frustie bristle) and then felt awkward when they waited on me. At home, I was used to clearing my own plate, helping to cook dinner, wash the dishes, or hang out laundry. If I tried to help out in Florida, Frustie snapped at me.

As a child, I didn't dare confront my grandmother, even though I was tall enough to look down on her when I reached junior high. It wasn't until I was in college that I finally challenged her. On one visit, in what had become a litany, Frustie spouted her usual theory about how "Barbie" (as she called my mom), "stole Dick away from Pittsburgh."

"That's a lie." I stood up abruptly, shaking. "Dad didn't *want* to join the family business. Just ask him. And if you ever speak about my mother that way again, I won't come back."

She stared at me, astonished—as if she'd forgotten whose daughter I was.

Grandpa was raised, in part, by his grandparents, who cared for Grandpa and his older brother, Carlton, after their father died. Their grandfather was an itinerant preacher, so they moved constantly, but the family always put a high value on education. Was Grandpa—who went to work as a young boy—uncomfortable having servants? I rarely saw him in the kitchen. That was Frustie's domain.

She's been dead now for more than twenty years, her mind destroyed by Alzheimer's. I remember her in the kitchen pantry, bent over a sink filled with snapdragons, hibiscus and greenery. Pieces of driftwood, smooth stones and shells collected from the beach are scattered on the counter beside her. Clippers and scissors snip, and intricate arrangements emerge from the tangle of color in the sink. By the end of the day, a single orchid is reflected in a flat mirror on a Chinese dresser. Delicate flowers wave from bud vases and small jars in the guest rooms, while a bold, tall vase of gladiolas stands on the baby grand piano. My cousin Katherine (who inherited our grandmother's green thumb) remembers that Frustie used her flower arrangements as models for her still-life paintings.

Frustie also had a landscape designer's vision. When she was president of the local garden club in Hobe Sound, she arranged for the planting of banyan trees along both sides of the main road leading from the drawbridge, the entrance to the island. Decades after Frustie's death, friends who own a condo in West Palm Beach drove us to Hobe Sound. I was thrilled to stop and walk under the arching canopy of those banyan trees. Their interlocking branches formed a majestic, green tunnel of shade over the road.

Frustie came to painting and sculpture late in life, studying sculpture at Carnegie Mellon in Pittsburgh. The Pittsburgh paper once featured Frustie's sculpture in a story titled *"Art takes bloom in classes at the museum"*—a profile that, sadly, I never saw until long after her death. The clipping shows my grandmother working with clay, seated beside the plaster statue she had molded of my cousins, Cabell and Katherine, their arms wrapped around each other. That sculpture later became the centerpiece of my grandparents' courtyard fountain.

Grandpa appreciated this statue, as well as another piece Frustie created for a second fountain: graceful seagulls that seemed to dip and soar in a spray of water outside the dining room. He humored Frustie's artistic endeavors, but sometimes his humor seemed close to mocking.

Though their Florida house was spacious, Frustie never had her own studio. She stored her paints and canvas in a closet that opened into the courtyard; not a spacious or healthy place to work with oils. (Did those fumes contribute to her Alzheimer's?) I asked her once why she didn't use one of the guest rooms as a studio—after all, they often sat empty— but she just shook her head. "It's better out here," she said, and retreated to her closet to finish a piece in time for her next painting class.

Frustie loved the endless round of parties that made up the winter's social circuit. Unlike my mother, who was late for most social events, Frustie was always dressed and ready well ahead of time. Her cocktail dresses were as petaled and filmy as the flowers she grew in her garden. While my grandfather dressed, she arranged herself on the piano bench, fluffed the tulle skirt of her party dress and launched into a string of show tunes. "Toot Toot Tootsie" was her favorite. She often followed that song with "I Could Have Danced All Night"—a sentiment she certainly shared. A fresh cutting from the bottlebrush tree trembled in a bud vase on the piano as her fingers tripped over the keys.

In spite of the comfortable life she led in Pittsburgh and later in Florida, Frustie longed for the time when four generations lived under one roof. "If only we were all living over the hardware store in Shreve," she said—an idea that gave me chills, once I'd seen the town.

Now it seems that her enthusiasm for life—her love of music and parties, her desire for art and beauty—were miracles. She overcame a split family, genteel poverty, a near miss with breast cancer that maimed one side of her body, her children and grandchildren living at a distance— and finally, the most devastating blow of all: the death of her adored husband. If she'd been born in my time, perhaps she might have attended art school as a young woman, then poured her love of color and design into sculpture or painting. She might have had a real studio, rather than a dark closet with no ventilation. Yet she went on, always hopeful and ready for the next dinner dance. She endured. Her flowers—and her art— sustained her.

The morning wind spreads its fresh smell.
We must get up and take that in, that wind that lets us live.
Breathe, before it's gone.
—Rumi

Sea Grape

Coccoloba uvifera

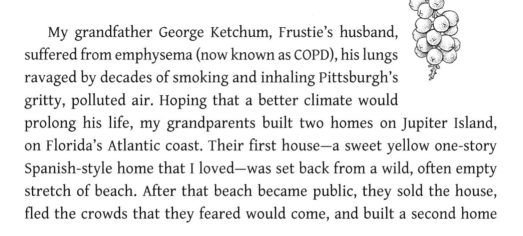

My grandfather George Ketchum, Frustie's husband, suffered from emphysema (now known as COPD), his lungs ravaged by decades of smoking and inhaling Pittsburgh's gritty, polluted air. Hoping that a better climate would prolong his life, my grandparents built two homes on Jupiter Island, on Florida's Atlantic coast. Their first house—a sweet yellow one-story Spanish-style home that I loved—was set back from a wild, often empty stretch of beach. After that beach became public, they sold the house, fled the crowds that they feared would come, and built a second home on a bigger plot a few miles south—still facing the ocean. Both houses had the same layout, with a central courtyard, a large living room, and bedroom wings on each side. We entered through a pair of heavy wooden doors, the only break in a solid wall that faced the parking lot.

When my brother and I were young, our family traveled to Florida on the overnight sleeper from Washington, D.C. We were sleepy and cross when the train pulled into the tiny station on the mainland, early in the morning. Grandpa picked us up and helped us wrestle our bags into his car's deep trunk. As we drove to the bridge that crossed the Inland Waterway to the island, I crossed my fingers and held my breath, praying the drawbridge would stay closed—even though, at other times, it was exciting to watch the mouth of the bridge yawn open, allowing boats with tall masts or fishing towers to pass beneath.

The drive to the house seemed endless after our rackety night on the train. The lush green of roadside plantings and the welter of flowers—hibiscus, bougainvillea, impatience—was almost overwhelming after a long, dreary winter. I could hardly wait to jump from the car when Grandpa pulled into the driveway. Heat radiated from the asphalt. Two enormous standing planters, filled with gardenias, flanked the front entrance. Their curled white flowers, bright against their glossy green leaves, gave off a sweet, almost cloying fragrance that grew stronger in the intense sun. Behind them, an enormous iron key gave the carved double doors an air of mystery and the promise of secrets.

As a child, it took all my strength to pull one door open. Stepping inside, I breathed in the delicious scent of the courtyard. Confederate jasmine climbed the corner posts, its sweet scent mixing with the smell of the sea. (Years later, the plant's common name made me squirm. Shouldn't the word "confederate" refer to something that smelled putrid?) The courtyard—filled with potted plants—was a cool oasis, away from the heat. Pots of pink begonias surrounded a central fountain, where water played over Frustie's sculpture of my cousins. The architect had designed the house so that the eye was drawn first to the wall of glass at the back of the courtyard, then through the living room and beyond, and finally to the plate glass windows with their dramatic view of the ocean. Whitecaps curled and beckoned over the gray-green water. The question was not *if* we would run to the beach, but *how soon*.

An old color photograph of my grandfather (Grandpa to me, Prr to my cousins) sits on my desk now. He's perched on the edge of a wrought-iron, cushioned chair in their Florida courtyard. *The New York Times* rests on the footstool in front of him, open to the editorial page. Sunshine slants across his thinning hair. Grandpa wears a short-sleeved button-down shirt, khakis, brown socks and lace-up dress shoes: formal attire for Florida but his version of casual. A tiny smile tugs at the corner of his mouth. Is he chuckling over a Russell Baker column?

Grandpa—who was always up on the news and had a keen political eye—seemed oblivious to the flowers and plants around him. As a child, I was intimidated by his intellect, his knowledge of world affairs, and his vast vocabulary. A men's group he founded, called The Whiz Kids, sounded comical but in fact, its members discussed politics, finance, history and current events.

Years later, I realized that his jolly friend Archie, a co-organizer of this group, was actually Archibald Roosevelt, son of Teddy—the president Grandpa most admired. When I was young, and in awe of my grandfather, I accepted his veneration of that president. After all, my Eurocentric American history classes, in both Junior High and High School, painted Teddy Roosevelt as a swashbuckling hero. It wasn't until college, when I studied with the Mexican American historian Ramon Ruiz, that I viewed our country's history through a different lens.

Looking back now, I wish I could have asked Grandpa: did he agree with Roosevelt's racist views? Did he approve of TR's international exploits? Did he see a contradiction between Roosevelt's conservation legacy and his passion for hunting wild game? I wish I'd known enough history myself back then to challenge him with those questions. But of course, no one in that house questioned my grandfather.

Though Grandpa teased me—drawing out my name with a *Liiiiza!*—he never put me down. I felt honored when he shared stories of his remarkable childhood. During my teen years, when we came to visit, he worked on his autobiography in the mornings. His furious, fast-paced typing clattered from his Florida office, at the far end of their house. Raised by his grandparents for many years after his father died, he wrote in his memoir that he'd learned to type and take shorthand—in order to work as a court stenographer after school—when he was "not yet eleven...and still in short pants."

His office was also where he was closeted with "that infernal machine," as he called it. He disappeared twice a day, hooking himself up to a pump that cleared his lungs and—supposedly—helped with his emphysema. Though our grandparents' wing was at the far end of the house, the rattle and hum of the machine, punctuated by Grandpa's terrible coughing, throat clearing and spitting, carried through two closed doors. It must have been wretched for him, but difficult subjects weren't mentioned in that house—so we all pretended not to notice.

Though plants surrounded Grandpa, inside and out, I don't remember seeing him with a trowel or a rake in his hand. The joke among our immediate family was that he couldn't even handle a screwdriver, yet he'd somehow piloted a flimsy plane in World War I. Granted, the technology was simple: a plane similar to the one he flew—on display at the Air and Space Museum in D.C.—looks like an enlarged balsa wood model with a joystick. Grandpa was a terrible driver, so it wasn't surprising that he'd crashed his plane twice over the French countryside during the war. According to Grandpa, during one disaster his plane plummeted from the sky into a haystack, where he grabbed a pitchfork and scrambled out of the pile. A frantic Frenchman, who witnessed a sooty creature emerging from the flames, ran away shouting, *"Le Diable! Le Diable!"*

Grandpa's stories about his time in France were light-hearted. He sang the tunes he learned in that conflict all his life, in his raspy, off-key tenor. "Beside a Belgian Water Tank"—about a pilot who "hung from a telegraph pole and...wasn't entirely dead"—was a family favorite. When I was older and read about the horrors of that conflict, I wondered if he'd held onto those songs as a way to forget the carnage he must have witnessed.

As a young man, he started a very successful advertising company, but in the years when I knew him best, he was partially retired. I thought of him as an intellectual, a storyteller, a gallant, courtly man whose gentle sense of humor charmed all ages.

So it was a shock when my aunt Janet told me, just before she died, that my grandfather's vision had shaped the gardens and grounds at their Florida house.

"But I never saw him actually *working* in the garden," I said.

"Oh no," my aunt said. "He knew what he wanted—and then he had it done."

He had it done. Indeed. A memory came back, probably during one spring break from boarding school when I visited my grandparents on my own. It was early in the morning. Grandpa stood in the wide expanse of yard that separated the house from the bluffs above the beach. Coconut palms, their slightly curved trunks crowned by a swirl of fronds, looked like graceful sentinels.

Grandpa and the Black gardener, who sometimes helped out in the yard, were studying a dead palm frond that dangled precariously above the house. Watching from the couch inside, I couldn't hear them through the plate glass windows—but clearly, Grandpa was handing out his instructions for the day. He was "having it done."

Now I wonder: Was he fair to this Black worker, who never came inside the house—or if he did, was he forced to use the back door? Did Grandpa—who certainly knew hardship growing up—pay him decently? Like so many questions about my grandparents, this one is lost to the past.

Past the formal yard, sea grape bushes grew wild along the bluff. Though my grandmother raised many exotic tropical plants in her garden, the native sea grapes were my favorites. Sturdy and low, they formed a natural barrier against storms and erosion. I loved the way their round, flat leaves, shaped like small dinner plates, clacked and rattled in the wind. The cool, sandy shade beneath the shrubs created a perfect hideout, while the heady scent of the ocean wafted from the breaking waves below.

One morning, Grandpa and I headed to the beach for the daily walk that helped to clear his lungs. He proudly led me to a wet spot under a sea grape bush to point out some large animal tracks. "A bobcat," he told me. Grandpa laughed when I gave him an astonished look. "Really," he said. "We have plenty of wildlife down here."

Of course, Florida wildlife also included poisonous snakes—which, thankfully, I never saw—and giant, furry spiders that terrified my brother and me. I never went to bed without first pulling down the top sheet, to make sure no creepy-crawlies lurked in the darkness.

Long before gardeners talked about the importance of native plantings, Grandpa was attuned to the natural relationship between sea and shore. While his neighbors built massive, expensive concrete seawalls to protect their properties from storms, Grandpa insisted that the sea grape bushes and native plants would hold the bank and prevent erosion. After one particularly stormy winter, he walked me down to the beach and pointed to his neighbor's seawall, the concrete gutted and puckered like crumpled egg cartons.

"Look at that mess. The neighbors were furious when I refused to spend forty thousand dollars on a seawall," he said. "Now they've got nothing— and we still have our beach."

Below us, the waves curled, paused and thumped against the hard sand. A great blue heron—a frequent visitor—patrolled the beach. Grandpa's eyes twinkled and he smiled: a rare hint of Schadenfreude? He was both a man ahead of his time, open to change and scientific discoveries—yet a conservative who believed that sometimes, the old ways worked best.

Fragrance, whether strong or delicate, is a highly subjective matter,
and one gardener's perfume is another gardener's stink.
—Katherine S. White
Onward and Upward in the Garden

Boxwood

Buxus sempervirens

Scents trigger memory. The smell of winterberry—crushed underfoot on a mountain trail overhung with pungent balsam—takes me to the High Peaks of the Adirondacks. The fragrance of lilacs evokes the evening in boarding school when Kay Herzog, our favorite English teacher, appeared at our dorm and whisked a group of us away to Boston's Arnold Arboretum, to experience the lilacs in bloom. What a thrill, to see Mrs. Herzog (as we called her), long hair falling loose from her bun, run through the grass among the abundant rows of purple, pink and white lilacs, as drunk on their scents as we were. And the slightly bitter, oily scent of boxwood evokes memories of the years we lived in Washington, D.C., near my beloved aunt and uncle, Janet and William Grayson.

I first encountered boxwood at Highlands—the estate that belonged to William's mother and stepfather, Mr. and Mrs. George Harrison—in Washington, D.C. I was five years old when my father took a job at the United States Information Agency. My parents sold our Vermont home, with its fireplaces tall enough for me to walk into, its yard that sloped to the Mettawee River, my chickens in their henhouse, and the homey kitchen where I played with our tomcat, Ralph. I was too young to understand why we moved. I didn't know that Dad's fledgling mail order business had failed. I only understood that we had left the only world I knew for a strange city. I'd said goodbye to our hens, who gave us our daily eggs; to our neighbors, the Hazeltons, and their horses; to Miss Hubble and her home kindergarten, where I made sand castles and painted happily at an easel—and to Weezie and Brook House.

In D.C., we stayed in a tiny apartment above the garage, next to my Aunt Janet and my Uncle William, who lived in Highland's carriage house. My memories from this period are slippery as shadows. While Mom and Dad searched for a place to rent, we were confined in the apartment's small, dark rooms. We ate at a wobbly table and at night, I covered my ears while Tom, my colicky baby brother, wailed. I dreaded each day in my new school, where a teacher belittled my attempts at the clay table and snatched the pencil from its comfortable spot in my left hand. After lunch, the boys bullied the girls on the playground, and the principal called me into her office to scold me for my daily stomach aches. "Stop imagining things," she snapped.

The garage beneath our apartment fronted onto a gravel driveway across from the main house, a stately stone mansion. There may have been gardens, but I only recall boxwood hedges lining pebbled garden paths. Freed from the horror of school and the darkness of our apartment, I ran between these rows, my skirt tangling at my knees, breathing in the sour smell of boxwood and celebrating my release. I kept a watchful eye out for Mrs. Harrison, a woman my father described, in slow French, as *form-i-dable*. I cowered beneath her critical, forbidding looks. Mr. Harrison, however, was warm, like my own grandfathers. I perched on his knee while he sang or told me silly stories.

Were the grounds of this estate on Wisconsin Avenue, as elegant as I remember? (The property later became the private Sidwell Friends School, so the Harrisons must have owned many acres.) We soon left the boxwood lanes and the tiny apartment behind, moving to a series of suburban and Northwest D.C. rentals, each more non-descript than the next. But our brief stay at Highlands was the beginning of a lifelong relationship with my adored aunt Janet and her husband William.

Like her mother, Frustie, Janet had a way with flowers. She was also a loving aunt, and passionate about dogs. Unlike my father, whose humor was laced with sarcasm, Janet had an infectious laugh and a playful warmth that made me feel loved and appreciated. When she and William bought their own house, on a lane that backed up to Rock Creek Park, they filled it with children—my three cousins—and critters. Where our only pet was Ralph, our huge, stolid tom cat, the Grayson's house boasted a menagerie. They always had at least two dogs. The ones I knew then were Flora, a border collie, and Sam Brown, a Norwich terrier. Uncle William, an avid birder, raised wood ducks in the bathtub. As my cousins grew, they had pet bunnies and once, a raccoon. All of these creatures—dogs, baby ducks and the occasional clutch of quail—rode with the family in their Nash Rambler on weekend trips to Blue Ridge, their farm in Virginia.

When we visited that farm, I felt as if I'd been freed from jail. During our years in D.C., my mother was still trying to pursue her career as a dancer. At night, I huddled under the blankets while my parents argued about Mom's evening rehearsals and performances. Dad was furious when Mom was out at night. I plugged my ears. Didn't she want to be home with us? Did Dad hate Mom's dancing? Would they get divorced?

Dad smoked incessantly. I didn't understand that his job at USIA was a nightmare, due to Senator Josephy McCarthy's investigations. Years later,

Dad told me that he never knew if he, or one of his colleagues, would be called before McCarthy's dreaded committee. Haggard men in gray suits often visited after dinner, disappearing into Dad's study through a haze of blue smoke. Their voices rumbled behind the closed door. So when the Graysons invited us out to Blue Ridge Farm, it was heaven.

The farm boarded brood mares: thoroughbreds that stayed at the farm during the months of their pregnancy and delivery. In spring, the mares grazed in the lush grass while their foals gamboled on their impossibly long, wobbly legs. In the evenings, I loved to walk through the long, white barns, listening as the horses snuffled the oats in their feed troughs or whinnied softly to their foals. I breathed in the heady mix of hay, manure, horsehair and worn leather.

The farm was also home to ponies, donkeys, chickens and beef cattle, plus a beehive that belonged to William's older brother, Gordon. When we were stung occasionally—since the bees lived next to the tennis court— Gorden just shook his head. "My bees don't sting unless you disturb them," he insisted. (Now that I have studied and written about bees, I realize he was right.)

Uncle William's wood ducks nested in the special boxes he'd built for them near the pond. And William often took us on spur-of-the-moment adventures. I remember a canoe trip where our keels scraped bottom as we paddled down Goose Creek. Another time, my cousins and I were squeezed into the back seat of William's Nash Rambler, rattling down a narrow dirt road near the farm, when he slammed on the brakes. We were all thrown against the front seats (no seat belts in those days).

"What's wrong?" my cousin Katherine cried.

"Look!" William jumped out of the car—leaving his door wide open. We scrambled after him. He pointed to a splash of red on the asphalt. "A scarlet tanager!"

We clustered around, forgetting we were in the middle of the road. The bird raised its head, flapped its wings and took off, disappearing into the woods. My chest hurt from bumping against the seat back, but we were all laughing. (So this was what it meant, I realized, to be a true birder.)

William's mother, Mrs. Harrison, was often at the farm, but somehow she didn't scare me as much there—perhaps because I lived outside and avoided the rooms where she presided. Instead, I tagged along after my aunt as she clipped flowers to arrange in tall vases, walked the dogs, or planned meals with her sister-in-law, Priscilla, and Sudie, the farm cook. Boxwood hedges—smaller than the ones at Highlands, but similarly fragrant—lined the paths outside the kitchen door. I can picture my aunt on the boxwood path, dressed for the garden in jeans and a faded button-down shirt. She stands with her hip akimbo, garden clippers in one hand, a cigarette (the cause of her eventual demise) in the other. Her blue eyes sparkle.

When I began to garden on my own, I realized that Janet had an eye for a garden's shape and layout. Something was always in bloom in her farm gardens. She was an artist like her mother: an accomplished painter who worked most often in watercolor. Her paintings featured gardens, flowers and country landscapes. A few years after our beloved, energetic uncle William died—far too young—of multiple myeloma, Janet remarried and moved to her new husband's home the next town over. Still in horse country, she transformed this garden, too. Its handsome terrace looked out on rolling pastures with the hazy ridges of the Blue Ridge Mountains in the distance. Close to the house, she created intimate walled gardens for herbs, flowers and vegetables. Low boxwood hedges also enclosed these beds. The scent of boxwood is stitched through my memories like a red seam in a chunk of quartz.

I associate Janet with the color blue: sapphire blue, like her eyes; the smoky blue of Russian sage (which thrived in her gardens but—for some unknown reason—won't grow in mine); the subtle bluegreen wash that graces one of her watercolor paintings, which hangs beside our bed at The Birdhouse; and the Delft blue of the tall delphiniums that anchored her handsome flower arrangements.

I'm grateful for the solace of that privileged farm refuge, where I escaped my parents' bickering and ran free. Without realizing it, I also absorbed William's love of birds. From my desk at The Birdhouse now, I watch goldfinches, cardinals and a hairy woodpecker land on our swaying bird feeder.

I soaked up Janet's appreciation for flowers and design. And every blue flower in my garden is grown in her memory.

I need no thermometer to tell me—
the rhododendrons are enough,
closed down like old umbrellas...
—Linda Pastan
It Is Still Winter Here

Rhododendron

Yakushimanum 'Ken Janeck'

In 1956, my father became the book editor at American Heritage Magazine and we moved from Washington, D.C. to Bronxville, New York, a suburb of New York City. We lived first in an old rambling house with a steep back yard and an ugly privet hedge. We soon sold that house and moved up the hill to a neighborhood called Lawrence Park. An artist's colony built in the 1920s, the Shingle Style houses, built with stone and heavy beams, boasted artists' studios, big libraries and intriguing play spaces. The families were as interesting as the houses, and my parents were soon part of a lively social group that the town's conservatives scornfully labeled "The Kooks on the Hill" or sometimes "The *Red* Kooks on the Hill." In those post-war, baby boomer days, most families had four or more children; five or six were the norm; a few families had ten or eleven.

In contrast, our family was unusually small, as was the house we bought: a split-level ranch tucked into a tiny yard. As soon as we moved, my brother discovered The Triangle, a small park a few blocks away, where the neighborhood kids played pickup games of touch football, baseball and kick-the-can. But I felt confined by our new yard. I was spoiled by our Vermont summers, where Sally and I were free to explore trails in the woods, search for deer in overgrown fields, or bike the four-mile loop around Dorset Hollow—all without adult supervision.

The Bronxville yard had a small lawn with a raised area at one end. Our back door opened into a narrow walkway shaded by a line of oaks. A rhododendron hedge ran along two sides of the yard. The mature plants, their trunks twisted with age, hid the house from the road. My parents liked the privacy, but I was antsy at first. The yard offered no trees where we could sling a hammock for reading; no secret places for imaginary play.

But Dad, as usual, had a vision for the yard's possibilities. He hired Ernest Marable, a gentle, strong Black man, who worked at the Otis Elevator factory during the week, to help out on Saturday mornings. Together, they transformed the brushy, sloping end of the yard into a terraced rock garden. In our first spring in that house, the rhododendrons bloomed. The blossoms opened to soft pinks, whites or flaming reds, and suddenly, we were popular. Strangers drove slowly past our house to view the colors, and neighbors included our yard on their evening dog walks.

Before long, I joined my family in referring to the rhododendrons as "The Rhodies"—as if they were part of the family, with unique personalities. On winter days, we used them to forecast the weather. When the temperature went below freezing, the rhododendron leaves curled and shriveled. "Hats and mittens today," Mom would announce, after a glance out the window.

Years later, when I was away at college and my brother was in high school, our parents put an addition on the house: a spacious living and dining area with a vaulted ceiling and tall glass windows that made the house feel part of the outdoors. When I came home from college, I was astonished by the transformation. But why expand the house, when I had left and Tom was about to depart? A teenage friend, living with us while his parents were posted overseas, had an astute theory—considering his age—about the addition: "When kids leave home," he said, "their parents either have a surprise baby or renovate the house."

Since Mom had been told that she shouldn't have more children, after two C-sections, his theory fit. But how to explain Dad's announcement that he planned to build a waterfall outside the sunroom's sliding glass doors? We teased him. A waterfall in *Vermont* was one thing, but in the suburbs? And *real* waterfalls didn't stop and start in response to a light switch. We called the setup "Dad's Folly"—until we saw that it actually worked.

The design was simple: a hidden pump forced water to the top of a small stone wall, where it cascaded over a ledge into a pool below. Rainbows sparkled as the water fell through sunlight. Birds flocked to the feeders and dipped in and out of the sheltered copse, using the pool as a birdbath. And the sound of the waterfall, when the doors were open, made a soothing backdrop for dinner conversations. Of course, the fountain froze up on the coldest winter days, and it could be temperamental, but Dad ignored our teasing. He loved watching the birds as well as the squirrels that came to drink there—much to the frustration of our collie shepherd farm dog, Shelley, who attacked the sliding glass doors headfirst, in a desperate attempt to catch them. (Though she was supposedly smart, Shelley never understood that the glass was impermeable.)

Dad planted roses beside the pool: the peace rose (*Rosa "peace"*) as well as a hybrid tea rose that we could never identify, which was a deep red, almost maroon. It reminded me of the solitary rose on Snow White's coffin in my book of fairytales. (In today's catalogs, it resembles "Always and Forever," a variety that claims to be hardy in Westchester County.)

Dad's delicate peace rose generally finished blooming at the first sign of a frost, shriveling up like a girl wearing skimpy party clothes in January. But his red rose wouldn't quit. It sometimes took a break after an early frost, but then had a second wind and bloomed late into the fall. One winter, when we were home for the holidays, rather than in Vermont, Dad pointed to the window on Christmas morning. A single red rose had blossomed overnight, its red petals in vivid contrast to the dusting of white snow on the bank behind it. Since I can't find the exact replica in catalogs or nurseries, I call it the Christmas Rose.

For years, Dad commuted to his job in New York City, riding the bus to the train station—or walking in good weather—where he was jammed into a crowded car full of fellow smokers. From Grand Central, he walked uptown to his office, where he read and edited manuscripts for the book division of American Heritage Magazine. I don't remember him complaining about the job—he did, after all, love history—but I do recall the way he looked every night at 6:45, when the town bus dropped him off at the end of our street. After Tom and I finished our chores and tidied the living room ahead of his arrival, I would run outside when I heard the bus groaning up the hill. Dad stepped off, carrying his briefcase, his face chalky above a gray suit that reeked of cigarette smoke. He'd welcome me with a half hug—"Hi, Miss Izey"—and we'd trudge up the hill to our driveway. Once inside, he found his drink—scotch on the rocks—waiting. Appetizers were laid out on the coffee table (cheese and crackers, or salted peanuts). Mom, freshly combed, a streak of fresh red lipstick on her mouth, had dinner simmering on the stove. Arguments were strictly forbidden.

At night and on weekends, Dad wrote books about the American Revolution, in part because that was his true love and calling, but also because we needed the extra cash. Since talk about money was "graveyard" (i.e. forbidden) in our family, I only learned years later that Weezie had paid my tuitions for summer camp and college, and that we lived beyond our means in this pricey suburb. Dad was under pressure at home and at work. So perhaps the garden, with its hardy rose and sheltering rhododendron hedge, gave him privacy, solace and a vision of the natural world he missed living in the suburbs.

American Elm

Ulmus americana

Like many towns and cities across the United States, Bronxville had its share of stately elms, the favorite trees for city parks and street plantings around the country. As a child, I loved our tree-lined streets. The branches of majestic elms were intertwined above the pavement like wedding guests lined up to create an arch for a departing bride and groom.

By the time we moved to Bronxville in 1954, the town's elms were already riddled with Dutch Elm disease, caused by an infestation of elm bark beetles. The town sprayed the elms with DDT on a regular basis. Rachel Carson's groundbreaking book on the dangers of this pesticide, *A Silent Spring*, had not yet been published. But my mother was wary of harmful chemicals and vigilant about our health. She had read Adele Davis's books on preparing and eating natural foods. Glass jars of homemade yoghurt proofed on our kitchen counter, and the milkman brought raw milk from a dairy in New Jersey. Mom's heavy wholegrain bread sent my brother running to the Ransom house a few blocks away in the mornings. (Since six Ransom boys jostled for food and attention at meals, no one noticed an extra boy snatching a piece of white toast on his way to school.)

The elms that shaded our small ranch house belonged to the neighbors on either side of us, who lived in three-story, stately houses with wide lawns. My parents weren't privy to their decision to spray their trees with DDT, believing they would kill the beetles. When the landscape trucks rumbled down our street, Mom went into panic mode. "Kids!" she cried from the front door. "Get inside! Close the windows! Lock everything!"

Tom and I—along with friends who were playing at our house that day—ran from room to room. We slammed doors and locked windows as the truck pulled up at the house next door. Mom followed behind, double-checking our work. Even with the windows closed, we could hear the hiss and smell the sickly-sweet odor as pesticide spewed from the hoses. The truck's powerful jets splattered the line of elms at our neighbor's, then turned to rattle the trees across the road. The men who wielded these hoses seemed unconcerned. They wore no masks or gloves, aiming their nozzles as if fighting a three-alarm fire.

"Your mom's crazy," my friend Barbara said, after she witnessed our routine.

Was she? The DDT trucks frightened me more than the "Duck and Cover" drills we had at school, where sirens wailed as we knelt on the basement floor, butts in the air, foreheads pressed against the concrete block walls, waiting for the All Clear. Those drills were preparation for an attack that *might* happen. The DDT trucks, on the other hand, sprayed a visible poison. When the assault ended, a sticky film coated our Oldsmobile and left a viscous sheen on the rhododendron hedge. The leaves of the elms, oaks and maples looked as if Jackson Pollack had splattered them with drips of gray and white paint.

Since cities relied on a monoculture of elms, rather than planting a diverse selection of trees, the beetles moved easily from one tree to the next. When Carson's *Silent Spring* was published in 1962, it showed that DDT *did* kill mosquitoes—for a while—but it also caused the deaths of thousands of birds. And DDT was harmful to humans. In spite of the spraying, Dutch Elm Disease continued to spread.

Meanwhile, my mother's vigilance and concern for the environment continued to the end of her life. In her seventies, she sat down in front of a bulldozer to protest the destruction of her beloved Vermont town green. (The green was saved.) A picture of a stranded polar bear or a poisoned wolf could cause her to weep—and reach for her checkbook, in case a gift to support wildlife might help.

Mom's activism, along with Helen Haskell's teachings at summer camp, left a deep impression on me. I have always gardened without chemicals or pesticides. A few summers ago, I spotted our neighbor across the alley from our city house, spraying a weed with a suspicious looking can. Dressed in a flimsy housedress and sandals, she stood on *our* side of the fence that divided our property from hers. "What are you doing?" I cried.

"Spraying with Roundup," she called back. "We have to get rid of this weed."

("This weed" was a small, innocuous-looking vine. It was *not* poison ivy; I'd already checked.)

"Glysophate is poison," I shouted, keeping my distance. "It's linked to the deaths of bees and butterflies and causes cancer in humans. There are children in this alley! It's dangerous for you, too! You should wear gloves and a mask."

Our neighbor stood her ground. "Roundup is completely safe!" she insisted. "It says so on the can." But she did turn off the spray before she stomped back to her own yard. We barely spoke again.

Like many daughters, I like to distance myself from my mother. I pride myself on the many ways that she and I are different. (Hah!) My mother had been dead a few years when I confronted our neighbor about her spraying, yet Mom might as well have been speaking through me.

Mom is on my mind at The Birdhouse these days, too. To my delight, John noticed—when we first purchased the house—that two elms were growing next to the fence, just outside our new yard. One was diseased, and we had it cut immediately. Yet the other, growing next to the road, was still healthy—at first. We chopped away at the brush and invasive plants that were choking its roots. Because a dying elm stood a half-mile down the road, and since Dutch Elm disease might have spread from the roots of the sick elm in our own yard, we guessed its years were numbered. Still, phoebes, sparrows and bluebirds flitted in and out of its branches every year, a marker of its health.

Then recently, on a clear July day, its leaves wilted, turned brown and began to fall. The dread disease had arrived.

A dead elm is almost worthless; its rigid wood is hell to split and it doesn't burn well. When the tree comes down, I won't be able to watch. I know its ghostly form will haunt that spot in the yard, and its memory will bring back my mother: her furious energy as she raced from room to room, protecting her chicks and teaching us to fight for the health and safety of all living things.

Everyone painted Dahlias—Renoir, Caillebotte, Monet.
What was it about the Dahlia? Color, I imagine,
and contrasting color and texture—the dahlia is wonderfully various.
—Penelope Lively
A Life in the Garden

Dahlia

Dahlia hortensis

Our family's move to Bronxville's
Lawrence Park, when I was eleven,
meant that we were suddenly part
of a vibrant, friendly neighborhood.
The Holland family lived across the street in a three-story brick home,
a neighborhood magnet for parties that always included music. The
Holland's living room was the heartbeat of the house. Two grand pianos
nested back to back at one end of the room, and instruments from every
corner of the world filled the spaces underneath.

Ken Holland was the director of the International Institute of Education. He and his wife, Mary, traveled constantly. They returned with instruments most of us had never seen or heard played. They made friends wherever they went, so their parties often included visitors from other countries, as well as foreign exchange students who were living with them or with nearby families—bringing some welcome diversity to our otherwise all-white town.

Everyone in the Holland family was musical. Mary and Kim, their oldest son, played piano. They could play anything, by ear or with music, from show tunes to folk songs to the latest rock and roll hits. (I later learned that Mary had supported herself, when she was young, by playing piano for silent movies.) Wendell, their sweet-tempered younger son, played drums; their two daughters had beautiful soprano voices. And Ken played the ukulele, which looked impossibly silly, propped on his round belly. No matter the occasion, someone always requested that he play— and sing—his version of "My Canary Has Circles Under Her Eyes," a tune that he claimed had only one verse. I looked it up recently and realized that Ken may have watered it down for this mixed age group, since the first verse goes:

Since making whoopee became all the rage
It's even got to the old birdcage
And my canary has circles under his eyes

Evenings at the Holland home began with a barbecue, with Ken at the grill flipping hamburgers and hot dogs. Casseroles, summer salads, deviled eggs and desserts filled a long table. The adults drank beer, wine and hard stuff while we kids dug sodas out of ice-filled tubs. Our neighborhood ran heavily to boys, who played catch with a baseball or a football on the sloping lawn until dusk sent everyone inside. Then the music began.

The instruments under the piano were available to anyone who wanted to try them. Strange warbles, deep oompahs, squeaks and vibrating twangs punctuated the music we made together as we gathered around the two pianos. Kim and Mary took their seats on opposing keyboards. Mary—who was tiny—occasionally craned her neck to catch her son's eye as they dove into a new tune. Sometimes she called out a key for the next number.

I watched in awe. How could they play in sync without seeing each other? Their hands danced over the keys as the adults—their voices lubricated by drink—called out requests. Bob Ransom, whose deep bass filled the room, taught us rounds, such as "Margery, Come Feed the Black Sow," and "Come Amaryllis to Thy Swain." Who—or what—was a swain? I had no idea, but their harmonies vibrated in my bones.

At some point—perhaps when I was in junior high—I realized that Mr. Holland (as I called him) was also a gardener. One afternoon, when I was searching for Marcia, the daughter closest to my age, I found Mr. Holland alone in the yard, tending his flowers. "Come see my dahlias," he said.

Thanks to my grandmothers and to Artie, I knew the names of many flowers, but I wasn't familiar with dahlias. I drew closer. The flowers were stunning: large and dramatic, with nests of whorled petals circling from a central nub. As he showed off different colors and varieties, Mr. Holland joked about their propagation and winked, as though including me in something risqué. I pretended to get the joke, but I didn't have a clue what he was talking about. For years afterward, whenever he saw me, he would mention his dahlias and raise an eyebrow, as if we shared a secret understanding. (Was this his version of the joke we shared in college, about boys who wanted us to "Come up and see their etchings?") Whatever the reason, Mr. Holland deserved to be proud of his flowers. The dahlias' bold hues stood out against the long green privet hedge running along its border.

I forgot about dahlias until the summer when my older son, Derek and his fiancée, Ali, were married in Vermont. I had offered to grow the flowers for their wedding ceremony and for the tables at the reception. My husband's uncle Jack, who grew dahlias, suggested they would hold up well. As I sorted through tubers in a local nursery, I remembered Ken

Holland (by then long gone). I pictured him in the garden, wearing faded Bermuda shorts, waving his clippers at me, a twinkle in his eye.

As promised, the dahlia's sturdy blooms added bold color to the table arrangements at the wedding. Now I can't garden without them. Dahlias were the pride of our city garden, where bright yellow "dinner plate" dahlias softened our neighbor's ugly chain-link fence. Pink dahlias nodded their heads in front of the buddleia; they towered over us as they reached for more sun.

Dahlias also thrive at The Birdhouse. In our early years, when other perennials were just getting started, the dahlias' vibrant orange and yellow suns nodded over newly tended soil. They stood up to a month of steady rain and wind. I have grown them every summer since.

In the fall, we dig up the tubers, set them in layers of vermiculite, and store them in a cool place. So far, the tubers have survived six winters. The voices of my parents' generation—all gone now—play in my head as our granddaughter K and I replant the dahlias each spring. We dig the holes with a small trowel. K settles the knobby tubers in the ground, and I remember my father and Bob Ransom (deep in his cups), leaning into one another on the bass line. After singing show tunes, spirituals and popular folk songs, darkness settles. It's time to go home. Dad and Bob Ransom sing the final song of the evening, which is always "Irene Good Night." Everyone joins in until the two men repeat the last verse alone, *a cappella*, to send us out into the velvet summer night.

Part Three
Breaking Ground

The best gardens are a perfect balance of order and chaos.
The tension created by this constantly threatened balance
is the pulse of the garden itself.
—Helen Humphreys
The Lost Garden

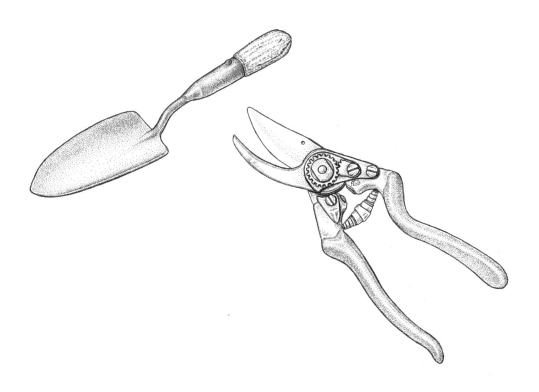

Oh, to be in England
Now that April's here!
—Robert Browning
Home Thoughts from Abroad

Beautybush

Kolkwitzia amabalis

In the summer of 1969, my first husband Casey and I spent a year in England. Contracted to write a book about British primary education, we stayed in London for a few weeks with my mother-in-law, Janet, until our research revealed that Oxfordshire boasted some of the most innovative schools in the country. Janet arranged for us to meet her close friend, Nancy Lancaster, who was willing to rent out a small cottage on her estate, known as Haseley Court.

We drove out to the tiny village of Little Haseley to meet our new landlady. She showed us around her massive main house, which was under renovation following a fire, and then took us to see the cottage, a small stone building covered with vines and climbing roses. Once a laundry, the cottage sat across from an identical stone building that had been the estate's brewery but was now an orangery, where pots of mock orange and jasmine spent the winter.

The cottage had four rooms—two up and two down—and was heated by the kitchen stove, a coal-burning Aga Cooker. With no insulation, the cottage walls were clammy through the English winter. Giant pale brown spiders (a particular phobia of mine) prowled in the corners and dropped onto the typewriter keys as I wrote, sending me screaming from the room. When the weather turned cold, the Aga's pipes banged and crashed in a brutal cacophony that required a visit from the local plumber. After a protracted consultation, he pronounced the pipes "furred," and needing careful attention. I can't remember now what he did to get rid of the "furring" except that it required him to spend long hours tromping up and down our narrow stairs. We served him at least one dinner and many cups of tea before the stove was finally fit to warm the house again.

But—and this turned out to be a huge *but*—the door of our cottage opened into acres of celebrated gardens. Eager visitors arrived in droves on the rare occasions when our landlady opened them to the public. Though we didn't realize it at the time, Lady Lancaster (as we knew her) was famous for creating—with her business partner John Fowler—what became known as "The English Country House Style." Before purchasing Haseley Court, which she brought back from near ruin, she had renovated Ditchley Court, where Winston Churchill sometimes stayed (in secret) when London was under bombardment, as well as the Kelmarsh estate. According to the Kelmarsh website, "Nancy Lancaster left her mark on Kelmarsh Hall's interiors, with the delicate terracotta coloring of the Great Hall, the exuberant Chinese wallpaper and seasonal flower arrangements." All three were stately homes, celebrated for their gardens' design and grandeur.

Lady Lancaster was quick to inform us about her less laudatory claim to fame: "I picked up my title from one of my husbands," she said. "You'll find that I've had far more success with butlers than with husbands."

As if to prove her point, Lady Lancaster's butler knocked on our door early one fall morning, holding a brace of pheasants. He thrust them into my hands before we could even wish him good morning.

"Madam said you would want these," he announced, and strode away. The dead birds were still warm; Lady Lancaster must have shot them at dawn. Luckily, the butcher in Thame, the nearby market town, was willing to clean and gut the birds for a few shillings. Sadly, the butcher hadn't removed the buckshot that nearly broke our teeth when we ate the cooked birds.

The niece and namesake of Viscountess Nancy Astor—the first woman to sit as a Member of Parliament in the English House of Commons—Nancy Lancaster was also a Virginian but had become as English as her aunt. "Haseley Court," she announced, "is my last garden."

Little did I know that I would make the same pronouncement about my own garden, more than forty years later. And I had no idea that, within a few years of meeting Lady Lancaster, I would struggle to create a garden where a scrim of acid soil barely covered granite ledges. If I could have foreseen the future, I would have followed this remarkable gardener as she worked her garden beds—and it was hard work indeed.

In spite of her title, Nancy Lancaster was indistinguishable from her staff during the day. Dressed in faded denim overalls, her hair in a wild tangle, shirtsleeves rolled to the elbow, she weeded, clipped and transplanted alongside her head gardener and his helpers; a trowel or clippers in one hand; a bushel basket full of weeds at her feet. A lit cigarette often dangled from a corner of her mouth.

Because we arrived in the fall, and because the cottage was a base for our travels to visit schools nearby and further north, I wasn't conscious of the gardens at first. I was amused by the chess garden, its greater-than-life-size pieces shaped from ancient box bushes. I admired the "Ha-Ha," an invisible ditch that kept grazing cattle from coming onto her lawn, while giving the false impression of level ground. (According to the writer Rebecca Solnit, this feature was "...so named because strollers were said to exclaim 'Ha! Ha!' in surprise when they came upon it.")

I liked to walk along the graveled paths when the staff had gone home. There I admired the gnarled, ancient wisteria arbor, as well as the fall lettuces, protected by cold frames in the kitchen gardens. The stone walls, covered in ivy, reminded me of the walls in *The Secret Garden*.

Our winter in Oxfordshire was cold, damp and dark. The sun disappeared by mid-afternoon. I had a bout with bronchitis that was finally cured by a week in Austria's crisp mountain air. Wrapped in heavy wool sweaters and hunched over our typewriter, we took turns writing our book.

And then spring came. When I walked in the small wood on the edge of Nancy Lancaster's property—an area I assumed was uncultivated—I discovered carpets of snowdrops poking through the leaf mold. Daffodils opened next in a host of colors, followed by Virginia bluebells. Soon, baby ducklings wobbled in the tall grass, following their mother to the canal on the verge below the wood, their peeps joining a chorus of frogs and spring birds. Though this area gave the impression of a wild woodland glade, it was as well planned as any of the more formal gardens.

Day by day, the gardens began to bloom, inside "rooms" created by the warm, yellowed stone. Each garden had a name: The Stone Garden. Old Vegetable Garden. Fruit Garden. White Garden. A central hub of perennials and boxwood connected the formal gardens. Most magnificent was a laburnum tunnel that ran outside the wall. Its cascade of yellow flowers formed an arch over a grass path ending at an ornate wooden bench.

One morning in April, when a friend from the States was visiting, we opened the kitchen door to a heady, sweet fragrance that almost knocked us over. An unassuming shrub on the doorstep had blossomed overnight. The scent from its tiny pink and white flowers was soporific and compelling. Our visitor—a landscape gardener—identified it at once. "*Kolkwitzia,*" he said. "Beautybush." We were drawn to the shrub like sailors pulled in by the Sirens in the Odyssey. I buried my nose in the flowers, then staggered away, overwhelmed. I hurried to the woods or strode between the figures on the chessboard, where the spicy, sharp smell of boxwood cleared my nostrils—and then returned to plunge my face into the bush again.

As spring progressed, the gardens showed more beauty each day. No sooner had one bed finished blooming than another began. Looking back years later, I wish I had pestered Nancy Lancaster with questions, or at least talked to her head gardener. (A gruff, intimidating man, he might not have welcomed my curiosity—but who knows?) I had so much to learn—about when and how to plant; how to orchestrate the garden for constant bloom; what to add (or subtract) from the soil; how to deal with pests and bad weather—in short, everything a gardener learns by trial and error. But I was young and had no garden of my own. We had a book to write, and a deadline. I'm left with regret as well as gratitude for those months of beauty.

I do a bit of research on *Kolkwitzia* now. The Proven Winners website describes her as a "Dream Catcher." Like so many shrubs and perennials, she was imported from China to England in 1901. Non-native, and a relative of the ubiquitous, invasive honeysuckle, she won't win a spot in our Last Garden in Vermont, but she does have a firm place in my heart. I will never forget the morning she bowled us over with her soporific fragrance, pulling us outdoors into the giddy, tipsy delight of an English spring.

Stones hold the heat, you know.
Oftentimes you can get a better crop off stony ground
than you can from soil that hasn't got any.
—Roger Leach, dairy farmer
interviewed by R.M. Ketchum, October 1991

Alice's Rose

Genus: Rosa Species: unknown

In the early Seventies, a few years after we returned from England, Casey and I bought sixty-two acres of land from a neighbor in Marlboro, Vermont. A scrubby piece of property with a young forest (cut over during World War II), and an overgrown field pock-marked with granite, its only attractive feature was a dramatic view of the mountains to the north.

Working with a friend who was an inexperienced architect, we broke ground during mud season. It was a chaotic year: Casey and I were both teaching, expecting our first child, and eager to put down roots. We lost track of the number of contractors and builders who worked on the house, and we ended up doing some of the finished work ourselves. We moved in—with Derek, our newborn son—after a November blizzard knocked out power and created frothy, impassable snowdrifts. When spring finally arrived, after a long, dark winter, it was time to do something about the yard.

I thought of Alice.

Alice Holway was a legendary gardener in Putney, Vermont. I had met her on a spring wildflower walk a few years earlier. Leading a small group into the woods near her home, Alice spotted flowers tucked so close to the forest floor that they were nearly invisible—at least to me. The names of plants slipped easily off her tongue. (I later learned that she had been a plantswoman, for more than thirty years, at Senator George Aiken's nearby nursery.) She introduced me to swamp pink. Shad. Pagoda dogwood. Hepatica nobilis, mayflower, wood anemone. Since Alice had mentioned that she owned a nursery and also designed gardens, I sought her help.

Alice drove up to see our new house on a cold, spring morning. The scene she encountered couldn't have been less promising. Marlboro is a forested mountain town with long winters and a challenging mud season. Our house, clad in raw cedar siding, perched awkwardly on top of a small hill, like a ship stranded on rocky ground. Bare soil, rocks, discarded lumber and torn Sakrete bags littered the muddy ground. Clouds of black flies swarmed as Alice stepped out of her beat-up car, wearing the beret that I later learned was her signature headgear.

As a garden site, our new property had everything going against it: at 1,700 feet, with a northern exposure, we'd have a short growing season. The heavy clay soil was acidic and shallow, a thin skin over granite ledge. The plot where we planned to start our vegetable garden faced south, but hardhack, ferns and stones were its current crop.

One pleasing feature was a new stone retaining wall, built to hold back the fill in front of the new house. Another plus was a pile of black topsoil that we had scrounged from the last farm on Route 5 in Brattleboro. The farm had finally succumbed to developers (who were creating the town's first shopping strip) and the departing farmers sold off everything—including their rich soil.

Alice was undaunted. With a few quick sweeps of her arms, she came up with a plan. We would create a perennial border in front of the wall. A row of low junipers would top the wall, to provide some green in the drab months and draw the eye away from the height of the new building. (Though she didn't say so, Alice probably agreed with me that the house was too imposing and exposed, with big plate-glass windows that faced north, and siding fastened at strange angles.) Alice said that a fragrant *Viburnum carlesi* would soften the northwest corner of the house, sending its sweet fragrance indoors. In the fall, its berries would attract birds. Alice was ahead of her time in pairing plants with birds, butterflies and other insects—the method that informs my gardening now.

"And I have the perfect rose for your front door." Alice's eyes twinkled until I could almost imagine beauty emerging from the mud.

We stood on top of the stone wall looking north, where clouds skimmed the blue-gray peak in East Dover. "What a lovely view," Alice said. She asked about flowers I liked. I told her I preferred pastel colors, and described both of my grandmothers' gardens: their perennials and shrubs. As we talked, a bird whistled a high-pitched song. "Listen!" Alice gave a bird-like tip to her head. "The white-throated sparrow," she said. "That call is so sweet and pure. You only hear it in wild, northern places."

The sparrow whistled again, a tune that bird books describe, rather prosaically, as "Old Sam Peabody Peabody Peabody." On that day, its call felt like a blessing.

Alice suggested I visit her garden in June, when the plants in her perennial beds would be ready to move. Meanwhile, I promised we would clean up the debris and stones that pockmarked the yard.

I soon learned that Alice was a long-time Leftie. In the Sixties and Seventies, she took in young people who needed a bed for a few nights, or a spot to regroup for a longer stay. Some described her place as a "communal boardinghouse." It was open to runaways, political exiles or dropouts from nearby Windham College. Some strays were back-to-the-landers (like us), in search of a place to put down literal as well as metaphorical roots; others had escaped from bad relationships or warring families. With a chuckle, Alice later told me that a few visitors had even bunked in her chicken house while others had set up a tepee in the back yard.

In exchange for a place to sleep and fresh vegetables from her garden, Alice pressed her boarders into service in the garden. She showed them how to divide plants, weed the vegetables, prune shrubs and start seedlings. Many of those early visitors and helpers became professionals in the community: teachers (as we were); community activists, therapists—even skilled gardeners themselves.

I drove to Putney on a warm day, weeks later, and followed the dirt road to Alice's nursery. The sign on her property announced: "Hemlock Hollow Nursery, Plants Rare and Choice, Visitors Welcome." A stony path led to the back door of the rambling farmhouse. The chaos inside was astonishing. Bulging backpacks and bushel baskets overflowing with fresh-picked, early spinach sat on the rough floors. Piles of progressive magazines and newspapers leaned precariously on every surface, and books were stacked everywhere. The Vermont poet Lynn Martin, who visited Alice in her later years, described her kitchen as "a big, old-fashioned plenty-of-room-to-can-hundreds-of-green-beans kitchen." This matched my own first impression.

But the house was not our focus. Alice greeted me, plunked her beret on her head, and led me outside. A shad tree was in full bloom at the back of the house, its delicate flowers quivering in the breeze. We picked our way among shrubs and fruit trees that looked permanent, though she told me they were for sale. Because our soil was acid, I chose a laurel and a rhododendron, in honor of my family's suburban garden, and some viburnums for the birds. I had told Alice about Brook House, and the row of highbush cranberries that separated the road from the yard. Her eyes lit up. "I helped myself to a beautiful cranberry on one of my forays around the state. Dug it up on the mountain between South and East Dorset. How about that one?" Of course, I couldn't resist a shrub pinched from my childhood town.

She also suggested mineral birches, to remind me of the birches that once arched over the stream at Brook House. We spent a long time among her perennials, where Alice pointed out her standards: the flowers clumped in her harum-scarum beds. I picked out familiar plants, not yet in bloom: peonies, bearded iris, phlox. She was surprised that I knew— and loved—the spikey *Baptisia australis*, with its stunning flowers and beautiful foliage. ("Better place it where you want it," she warned. "It hates to be moved.") Her eyes widened when I asked for two fraxinellas (*Dictamnus albus*), also known as the gas plant. "They may give you a rash," she warned.

I knew that—but fraxinellas had thrived in my grandmother's garden, and Weezie was still alive. Though she no longer owned Brook House, maybe these flowers would trigger happy memories.

After Alice scribbled a list, she took me around the corner of her house. I gasped. A wall of delicate white roses covered the side of the house like a curtain. Branches arched over the windows and twined across the siding, reaching the eaves. It reminded me of the twisting vines growing up Rapunzel's tower, in an illustration from my mother's book of fairytales.

Alice laughed when she saw my face. "This is the rose for your front door," she said. "Don't worry; you can keep it in check. It comes from northern China. It doesn't mind cold, wind or rocky soil. It will thrive in your setting."

Really? I was skeptical, but Alice was convincing—and she certainly knew more about plants and their habits than I did.

Alice and her crew arrived on a day swarming with black flies and mosquitoes. They disembarked from rusty cars, shovels in hand, ready to plant. I watched nervously, carrying our baby, Derek, on my hip, as Alice's crew lugged boxes of limp, woebegone plants from a Jeep. Alice was the stage director. She placed each pathetic plant on a lonely spot of pock-marked soil, gave a series of friendly orders (inaudible to me), and then watched as her crew began digging. They filled each hole with compost before setting the plants in the ground. Shovels clanged against rocks, but Alice chuckled. "Rocks are part of the soil," she said. "I usually leave them unless they're really in the way."

When the new perennial border was planted, Alice held up a piece of her rose—a spindly tangle of root and canes—and instructed her helpers to plant it in the angled corner beside our front step. I rolled my eyes at the young woman who set the pathetic canes on the ground, to show my skepticism—but she slammed the shovel into the hardpan and gravel, tossed it onto burlap sacks, and settled the canes into black compost.

A few hours later, our new yard—such as it was—boasted a few scraggly shrubs, a row of small junipers, and some sad, spindly perennials with grass tangled in their roots. Hard-packed dirt, where grass seed had yet to sprout, surrounded the mess.

"Don't be alarmed," Alice said, as if guessing my thoughts. "Everything will fill in. You'll learn about gardens, your friends will share their extras with you, and soon you'll be dividing your own things and giving them away."

She was right, of course. But I wasn't so sure about the rose. It didn't bloom for a few years and its feathery new growth, each spring, concealed tiny, razor-sharp thorns. I was about to give up and plant something more reliable, when a few buds the size of my pinky fingernail appeared one early June. The flowers opened on my birthday. Their white petals stood out against the graying cedar siding. Within a few years, the rose would help me celebrate every birthday with masses of blooms, the roses so thick they hid the foliage. Remembering how the shrub had taken over Alice's house, I cut it back each year after the blooms were finished. The petals fluttered in the wind and gave off a delicate scent. For the few weeks that the rose was in bloom, it was spectacular.

But the flowers were fragile; they gave way in a strong wind or downpour. For the rest of the year, the rose was rather ordinary. It grew fast and leggy if left untended. Properly pruned, it had a pleasing inverted umbrella shape, like that of an elm—but it needed to be reined in. It required pruning twice each summer, which meant putting on heavy gloves and a long-sleeved shirt, finding a sturdy stepladder, and submitting to clipping torture. If the rose were a family member, she would be my cousin Kezia, who died far too young: a tall, striking beauty, highly creative, yet prickly and challenging as all get out.

Before long, I started sharing pieces of the rose. Two small stalks that I gave my parents became the vase-shaped shrubs framing their front door, giving it a less formal look.

In spite of our warnings that it could take over, Alice's rose was popular with anyone who witnessed her stellar performance in June. I gave canes to many friends, including talented gardener Randy Hesse, who took a piece of the rose when they left their home in Williamsville. When the Hesse's home—and its garden—washed away in Hurricane Irene, the rose's daughter was already flourishing in their new yard.

After my first marriage ended and I left our Marlboro home for good, I took a piece of the rose with me. Its prickly thorns and ephemeral beauty will always remind me of Alice—and of the home we created for our family.

The gladness of green growing things is apparent to the seeing eye.
They rejoice with a radiant joy.
—Celia Thaxter
An Island Garden

Vegetables

From the Latin: Vegetāre-To enliven

The perennial border wasn't
the only garden we created from scratch in Marlboro. From the moment
we purchased the property, I knew we would have a vegetable garden.
We were starting a family and wanted our children to have healthy food
grown on our own land.

Though it's been decades since I last buried my hands in that cold
soil, the record of our work exists in my oldest garden journal: a battered
green, three-ring binder filled with cramped, tightly written notes—my

twenty-five years in a hill garden. If I open the notebook now, it emits a musty smell and a flood of memories.

Starting in 1973, our first summer, I drew detailed maps for each garden year. I kept careful track of vegetable and herb varieties, and noted frost dates, both the last frost of the spring as well as the first frost of the fall. Sometimes a frost arrived in June, freezing tender seedlings. One August, I note that we were madly covering tender plants at dusk, then rising at 4 a.m. the next morning to water; desperate to save our tomatoes, cucumbers, beans and basil. In my journal I also commented on weather, especially extreme events. "Four inches of water standing in the corn rows this morning," or, in contrast: "Dry dry dry summer. Where is the rain?" An early summer entry might mention slugs drowning in the beer traps I'd set among the strawberries—followed by jottings, a month later, that we'd picked and trimmed and eaten—and frozen—many quarts of these same delicious ripe berries.

The actual work of creating a vegetable garden in that cold, mountain town was daunting and backbreaking. As soon as the snow melted after our long first winter in the new house, we laid out our future garden with stakes and string, then waited for a neighbor to arrive with his tractor. Black flies fluttered in ominous clouds as the tractor carved deep furrows. The blade shuddered in the heavy clay soil.

My heart sank. The plow's blade uncovered bushels of loose stones and small boulders—not a surprise in a landscape gouged by glaciers over thousands of years. But the blade also clanged against seams of granite ledge that ran along each side of the plot. Our first soil test, sent to the University of Vermont extension service, confirmed what we had learned from our neighbor friends, Diana and Francis, who had gardened nearby since the end of World War II: the soil was extremely acid, lacking in nitrogen and other minerals. A stand of white pines protected the garden from the prevailing northwest winds, but the plot was in Zone 3, at 1,700 feet. It was an inauspicious beginning.

And we were busy. Derek, who was still nursing, wobbled in our flimsy backpack carrier as I tossed stones from the upturned soil. When we ran out of money for the finished work on our new house, we sent the construction crew away, leaving us to put up trim and paint bedrooms ourselves. We had purchased one goat—a cranky white Saanen we named "Permelia," after a famously irritable friend of my grandmother's—and we were looking for another goat to keep her company. Casey was teaching sixth grade while I was meeting with a group of parents eager to help me start a nursery school. Did we have time for a vegetable garden?

Still, we were young, and determined to grow and eat food free of pesticides. I had memories of raising fresh vegetables with my mother, as well as under Helen Haskell's guidance at summer camp. We had manure delivered the first year. In later summers, manure from our own goats, as well as a small flock of sheep, added fertility to the soil. We tilled in lime, tossed out stones, swatted black flies, experimented with hardy varieties, hauled away more stones, slapped at deer flies.

Each year, I bought garden books. Sam Ogden's *Step-by-Step to Organic Vegetable Growing* became my dog-eared resource for many years. Like us, Sam gardened at altitude and understood Vermont's challenging conditions. (More than forty years later, when it's time to plant the garden, I still turn to Ogden's book, though it's warped and yellowed with age, and printed in a hard-to read two-column format.)

From Ogden and other gardeners, I learned about companion plants and organic pest control—which sometimes worked, sometimes failed miserably. We discovered that raised beds helped to drain our heavy clay soil and warmed the earth sooner in the spring. When varmints of all kinds—rabbits, woodchucks, raccoons and deer—devoured our tender seedlings, as well as ready-to-pick corn, we gave in and put up electric fence.

Digging the asparagus bed was the hardest work of our new garden, but we had been inspired by our friends Francis, a sculptor, and Diana, a painter, whose gardens were also works of art. Their asparagus bed, laid out behind their old farmhouse, yielded bunches of fresh, green spears that poked up through blankets of bleached straw each May. Diana and Francis had shared their bounty with us when we had rented the one-room schoolhouse at the start of their road. Asparagus was one of my favorite vegetables, so of course we would start our own bed.

Diana had warned us, in her dry voice, that making the bed would be arduous, but we didn't pay much attention until we staked out the proposed plot. Our neighbor's heavy plow had turned over the sod. Now our pitchforks strained against the wet clay as we tried to loosen the soil. We piled big stones beside the garden, screened out smaller ones, and added compost. The plants came in the mail tied up with string, looking about as healthy as a collection of dead, dangling spider legs. We fanned out the roots, covered them with screened soil and waited, that next spring, for the first tender shoots to appear. The second year, we cut a few slender stalks or ate them raw in the garden. It wasn't until the third year that we could actually cut enough asparagus for a meal. For that, we had a celebration.

One summer a few years later, our dear friend and neighbor Patty Webster joined forces with me in the garden. By now, Casey and I had a second son, Ethan. The Websters also had two boys, so our four sons were like stair steps, each a year apart, from Jason—the Webster's oldest—to Ethan, our youngest. The Websters lived down the road in a nine-month rental that they had to vacate every summer, so they needed a place to garden. While Patty and I weeded, thinned and cultivated, the boys played in the sandbox Casey had built just outside the fence, pushing their Tonka trucks, backhoes and bulldozers through wet sand.

It was fun to experiment with new plants. I'd never heard of Jerusalem artichokes, which Patty and I planted eagerly (only to regret it when we discovered that they were thugs, poking up in every corner of the garden). We grew unfamiliar herbs, such as coriander and feverfew. We started a strawberry bed, with runners that Patty carefully trained with bobby pins, setting out tins of beer to attract (and drown) the slugs. Recently, I reminded Patty of that summer. "That was the year you taught me how to garden," I told her.

"Oh no," Patty insisted. "I was learning from *you*."

Was this the summer of the first *Moosewood Cookbook*—the year many of us cut down on eating meat; the year we had potluck dinners where four or five couples cooked from those recipes, using ingredients from our own gardens? (My attempt to make "The Enchanted Broccoli Forest" flopped when the spears refused to stand up like trees.) In my journal, I noted that Derek had his own garden the year he turned six—was that when Patty and I gardened together?

As the vegetable garden was established, we also grew fruit. Looking through that old garden notebook, I find a bill from Alice Holway for "25 strawberry plants @ .10/each. 25 raspberry canes @ .25/each." (Only a quarter per cane! They're now at least $5 apiece in most garden catalogs.) Those raspberries filled two long rows outside the garden, while strawberries grew in a raised bed inside the fence. Both fruits were prolific and happy in that acid soil, as were the blueberry bushes (also from Alice) that we planted along the back fence.

In my journal, I kept track of garden successes: Silver Queen sweet corn when our Harwell cousins visited from Nashville; so many tomatoes that I spent long hours in the steamy kitchen, fans blasting as I canned them whole or cooked and froze their sauce. We picked colanders full of beans, enough for a big batch of pickled dilly beans to pucker our mouths in the winter.

As I turn the pages of my old notebook, a clutch of 3x5 cards tumbles out. Blue stars announce first prize awards for our vegetables at the town fair. How fitting that the Latin source of the word—vegetables—comes from the verb "to enliven."

There were also garden disasters. The worst was the discovery that one summer's carrots, layered in sand in a deep wooden crate, had rotted from top to bottom in our root cellar. They oozed a disgusting orange paste when I dug into the sand to pull out a clutch for an autumn dinner. I screamed in despair, and Casey clattered down our basement stairs, expecting a medical emergency. My journal also notes a blizzard that arrived on April 7th one year, deep enough to cover the picnic table in our back yard—as well as the peas I had just planted. Another entry mentions a frost one August 29th that left me with bags of green tomatoes. As in all gardens, there were pests: Japanese beetles, slugs, cabbage moths. And Alice Holway's fruit trees were a bust at that altitude. Her plum and apple trees rarely flowered and never bore fruit.

Our family's private story is hidden in the garden notebook. As Derek and Ethan grew up, it was harder to get their help in the garden. They went to summer camp, then high school in the next town, where they were involved in sports and afterschool activities. They had summer jobs repairing bikes, mowing lawns, washing dishes at the local inn. They made new friends in high school and brought them home on weekends, filling the house with male energy and noise. The boys disappeared into the woods skiing or mountain biking; took daredevil sled rides on steep icy pastures; built hideouts in the forest; introduced us (awkwardly) to their first girlfriends. I could never grow enough food to feed their teenage appetites, but we loved having their friends at the table. Then they went off on wilderness adventures and applied to college. They were leaving home—which was appropriate, though heartbreaking. It was their time.

As they left and came back, left and returned for shorter stays, our marriage was unraveling. That tale isn't spelled out in the notebook—but now, leafing through those pages, I find it buried in what is left unsaid. The truth is like invisible ink that requires lemon juice to reveal the words hidden beneath. Where once I was meticulous in noting vegetable varieties, their successes and failures—even creating a crude early spreadsheet on the first computer I owned—my notes were cursory in the last three years of the garden. In the past, I carefully ruled out my garden maps and labeled each row with dates of planting and harvest. Years later, my penciled scrawls were hard to read. In 1992, my last full summer in Marlboro, we planted half the garden with a cover crop of buckwheat. With the boys away, we didn't need to fill the freezer, root cellar and cupboard with our harvest. To my astonishment, I see that I even planted a meager garden the year I moved out—perhaps because I couldn't bear to see the plot grow up to weeds, perhaps because I lurched between leaving and staying.

Our mountain garden sustained us for two decades. And it nourished me spiritually. It anchored me in times of sorrow and gave me joy when we put fresh, healthy food on the table throughout the year. Yet in the end, it could no longer feed my body—or my soul.

The original property that we bought in Marlboro—62 acres—was bordered on two sides by a woodlot owned by our neighbor, Bill Davisson. A network of trails and logging roads ran up and down the hills of his forest. Bill owned a few pairs of glossy, high-stepping horses, as well as a collection of antique carriages, which he drove along his woodland trails. Deep in those woods, halfway up a steep hill, his horses would stop to blow near an old cellar hole. Years earlier, perhaps during World War II, some family had farmed on that spot. (Legend had it that "the ghost of the Widow Ball"—whoever she was—still haunted that clearing.) In our time living nearby, birch trees thrust up from the cellar, and an ancient lilac flowered in what must have been the dooryard, matching Amy Lowell's description of a long-neglected homestead: "Lilacs, wind-beaten, staggering under a lopsided shock of bloom/Above a cellar dug into a hill."

I was alone at the house the morning I left for good. I threw my arms around our black lab, sobbing into her fur. She pulled away, head down, as if she already sensed my betrayal. I climbed into my car but couldn't glance in the rearview mirror, for fear that the garden—and its memories—would pull me back. Would our plot of ground, following old-field succession, revert to hardhack and ferns, then to aspen, birches and white pine; eventually to mature forest? Would the occasional spear of asparagus poke up through packed soil, to show new owners that gardens once flourished in that northern plot of ground?

A piece of my heart, like a shard of broken glass, remains in that abandoned, rock-strewn soil.

I took my money and bought flowering trees...
The red flowers hang like a heavy mist;
The white flowers gleam like a fall of snow.
The wandering bees cannot bear to leave them;
The sweet birds also come there to roost.
—Bai Juyi
Planting Flowers on the Eastern Embankment

Zumi Crabapple

Malus X "zumi"

During four long years of personal upheaval and constant moves, I lived without a real garden. But in May of 1997, a year after John and I were married, we bought a house in Watertown, Massachusetts. The house—one of the few single-family homes in an Armenian neighborhood of double- and triple-deckers—was on a narrow alley that was hard to find (no GPS to guide us then). The tall, skinny, three-story blue house—clad in asbestos siding—was not an ideal choice. The young architect who had bought it at an estate sale hadn't finished the renovations. He had a good eye: he had opened up the boxy rooms on the first floor, enlarged the front porch, and was in the process of turning the attic into a usable space. (He was also a novice builder, something we didn't realize until John just missed grabbing a bare, high-voltage electric cable that the architect had neglected to cover.)

The house sat on a postage stamp yard, flanked by a chain-link fence on one side and a paved driveway on the other. An old wooden fence at the back leaned over a narrow garden—choked with English ivy—and a narrow concrete walk.

But it was the "House of the Week" in the Boston Globe's Real Estate section one Sunday. We were intrigued by the story—"Young architect brings an old house back to life"—yet dismayed to learn, from our agent, that the house had sold the moment it went on the market. However, it came up again on listings the next week. Apparently, the first deal had collapsed.

We hurried to the second open house and joined a crowd pushing up the stairs and peering into the rooms. "Nice house, but no closets," a number of women said, as we looked around. John and I glanced at each other and raised our eyebrows in silent agreement. No closets? No problem. The house sat on a small hill, which gave it a view and—even better—lots of sunlight. We were drawn to the tall windows, the high ceilings and bulls-eye molding, and the open plan on the ground floor. The renovated attic faced south and looked out over backyard gardens and the tops of shade trees: a perfect writing studio for me. We rousted our grumpy real estate agent out of his girlfriend's bed and made an offer. Within a few days, we were on our way to ownership.

The house had some issues, of course—what century-old house doesn't? But the yard would be our biggest challenge. While the obstacles in my first Vermont garden had been natural—poor soil, northern exposure, ledge and critters—those we faced in Watertown were manmade. Concrete curbs held back empty flowerbeds. The architect had filled a small garden plot at the side of the house with uneven rows of puny arborvitae, as if to start a forest. In an L-shaped corner beneath the dining room, we discovered an enormous, twisted tangle of roots. I shuddered in dismay when Henrietta, our new neighbor, told us that the architect/builder had chopped down a big lilac there. "That shrub was as old as the house," she told me. "What a shame. He said it was 'in the way.'" She shook her head in disapproval.

Even worse, torn roofing shingles, metal staples, nails, broken glass, rebar and chunks of concrete from the construction littered the ground around the house. When I stuck a trowel into the ground along the chainlink fence, I uncovered a line of bricks buried deep in the soil. (The remains of a former property boundary? Who knows.) But Henrietta told us that the long-time owner, who had lived in the house until her death, grew roses along the wooden fence at the back. In spite of the tangle of dead canes and ivy, the first blush of leaves was showing among their thorns. "She grew so many roses," Henrietta told us. "And they were beautiful. Just beautiful." Buds swelled on two low azaleas and a healthy yew helped to hide Henrietta's throbbing AC unit. Could we create an oasis in the midst of concrete and pavement? It would be a challenge— but hadn't I started from scratch once before?

First things first: the yard needed a tree. In fact, there were few trees in the neighborhood. Many of the streets' narrow planting strips had been paved over to make more room for cars. A big ash grew on the property line behind our new house, its roots buckling the pavement of a nearby driveway, while an enormous silver maple shaded the house at the end of the alley—but the only tree on our lot was a puny, twisted pear, growing near the back door. Our Vermont friend Ahren Ahrenholz, a skilled craftsman, potter and landscaper, suggested planting a crabapple off the corner of the front porch. He pulled up a few days later with a lovely big tree in the back of his pickup.

It was a Zumi crabapple, a variety unfamiliar to us. Ahren promised we would like its form and flowers. Digging a deep hole and planting it was hard work. The tree was heavy, with a wide root ball; our soil compacted and full of debris. John bought pressure-treated railroad ties to hold the earth we had hauled in to create a decent bed around the tree.

For a while, the tree looked spindly and spare. My notes for the following spring—when it finally bloomed—mentioned that it had survived "the dual traumas of windburn and drought." At first, I was lukewarm about its flowers. "Its blossoms are fragile and pale, like roses blown apart too soon," I wrote—but my scrawl in the margin, written two years later, was enthusiastic: "I have learned to adore this tree."

The vegetable garden was another story. When we first moved in, I told my friend Prosper that we hoped to grow vegetables in the tiny plot of soil on the east side of the house. Prosper, a Mainer who was now raising tomatoes in Somerville, advised us to test for lead. She explained that before she bought her tomato plants, a friend had warned her about high lead content in city soils. Prosper had her soil tested and found the lead content was off the chart—so she raised her tomatoes in pots.

John—who knew about lead poisoning from his pediatric practice—agreed with Prosper. "In the country, lead from house paint can wash out and dissipate," he told me. "In the city, it stays trapped between the buildings."

I ordered a test kit from the University of Massachusetts Extension service, gathered samples from the beds next to the house, as well as from the proposed veggie garden, and sent them off. Sure enough, the results came back with bold print warnings about the dangerous levels of lead in all our soils, and the steps we should take to ameliorate the problem.

The report was daunting, but we were determined to have a garden. We decided not to treat the soils next to the house, since we didn't have children or pets (this was years before our first grandchildren were born). We would have to clean our shoes and tools after working in those beds. As for the vegetable patch, we needed to remove the soil and start from scratch. Looking through my garden journal from that time, I find this note, written on May Day, 1998:

The transformation has begun: from urban, lead-filled rigid "soil," filled with lumpy concrete, broken glass, wires, and lead—to urban cottage garden. Owen—he of the Bobcat—arrived on Tuesday to haul away the lead soil and replace it with organic loam (pronounced "loom" around here). We have created massive amounts of work for ourselves, and the garden is still a figment of our imaginations—but we hope to create an oasis in the midst of concrete, chain-link fences and triple-decker homes.

As with all gardening, our vision changed as we aged and our family grew. Twelve years after buying this house, we were blessed with the arrival of our first pair of grandchildren, first a boy, R, and then, three short weeks later, a girl, W, born in Arizona. Soon after our grandson was born, R and his parents moved to Boston. When he could toddle outside, I included him in the garden cycle by growing pumpkins. We chose varieties from Johnny's seed catalog and from the first, R fell in love with the big white "Polar Bear" variety—which turned out to be excellent for carving. We planted the seeds in April. He spooned soil into the peat pots, poked them into the soil with his tiny fingers, and watered them carefully. We set the tray of pots in a sunny window, then transplanted them into bigger pots after their second leaves opened.

After the soil had warmed outside, we dug small holes and planted the seedlings tenderly in the garden. When R's little sister, K, reached the same stage, she chose traditional orange pumpkins ("Racer" was a favorite) and our trays of seedlings expanded. Once established, the vines crowded out everything else, sometimes snaking out of the garden and onto the sidewalk, like some prehistoric, cartoon vine. We never had many ripe pumpkins—but the kids were excited to have their own Jack-O-Lanterns. And I loved sharing nature's cycle with them—from seed to flower to fruit to harvest. Soon they were old enough to circle their favorite varieties in the catalogue, to break up the soil and hill it up at planting time; to label the wooden stakes that marked the plants.

As the children grew, so did the Zumi crabapple. Our vegetables struggled to compete with the tree's spreading shade and roots. After we purchased The Birdhouse, we grew most of our vegetables in Vermont. And my interest in the city garden changed. I joined our town's newly formed "Friends of Bees" committee, and learned more about plants that attract pollinators. Our members drew up lists of pollinator plants, as well as nurseries that sell plants without neonictinoids: the harmful pesticides linked to the collapse of bee colonies. Each year, I added more beneficial plants, until our gardens trembled with bees: honeybees, bumble bees and other wild native bees became regular visitors.

When we started our city garden, my goals were both personal and practical. I struggled with drought, concrete and pulsing summer heat to create a haven of privacy, beauty and color in a city neighborhood. Later, as I learned about the devastating losses of bees around the country, as well as the monarch butterfly's risk of extinction, I was happy that our urban garden provided a small oasis for birds and pollinators. At summer's end, monarchs often visited our garden, fluttering between the fall asters and the Joe Pye weed, gathering strength for their journey south. Our grandkids, who studied the monarch's cycle in school, understood my excitement when monarchs visited our garden, as well as their own.

As for the Zumi, the once spindly crabapple became a mature tree. For me, spring arrived along with the male cardinal, who usually appeared just before the Zumi's buds opened. He would sing his heart out for days, waiting for his mate. She would waltz in fashionably late in order to choose the best spot for their nest—often hidden in our inkberry hedge.

Some mid-April morning I would open the door to find the Zumi's abundant flush of pinkish-white flowers standing out against its dark green leaves. I would stand beneath the tree, breathe in its fragrance, and listen to the hum of thousands of bees. I was as drunk on the nectar as on the beauty of the blossoms. On hot summer nights, the tree's thick branches gave us shade and privacy as we sat on the porch, waiting for a breath of cool air. In the fall, cardinals, robins and sparrows flitted in and out of the branches, feasting on the bitter yellow crabapples before flying to the birdbath in the back, where they fluttered and splashed. And in winter, wet snow clung to the dark branches, evoking a Japanese print. I knew that—if and when we ever sold this house—it was the tree, rather than the gardens, I would miss the most.

Then I step out into the garden, where the gardener,
who is said to be a simple man,
is tending his children, the roses.
—Mary Oliver
The Gardener

Alice's Rose, Redux

Genus: Rosa Species: Unknown

Soon after John and I created our Watertown garden, I dug up shoots of Alice's rose in Vermont and transplanted them on the corner of our city property. I hoped that the rose would provide color when it blossomed in June, and that it would hide our neighbor's ugly chainlink fence, which ran along one side of our tiny yard.

The rose had an inauspicious beginning. When I started to dig a hole for planting, my shovel clanged against buried bricks. We wrestled them out—along with broken glass and crumbled concrete—and filled the hole with compost. I set the rose cuttings in place, holding them up with bamboo poles—and watered often. The rose struggled for its first two summers, then suddenly began to thrive. Apparently, she didn't mind the heat that rose in waves from blacktop in the summer, or the piles of snow thrown up by the plow in winter. She grew bushy and began to hide the fence—just as we had hoped.

When I first moved to Massachusetts, I was introduced to Robin Wilkerson, a master gardener, horticulturalist and landscape designer who has become a close friend. As our city garden began to take shape, I asked her to draw up a plan for our yard. One May morning, Robin pulled up in her pickup truck, looking very much like a Vermonter, with her long braid and wide-brimmed hat. She stepped out, took one look at our fence, and gasped. "You've got Alice's Rose!"

Robin had lived in northern Vermont before her marriage—and like so many gardeners from the sixties, seventies and eighties, she was drawn into Alice's vortex. Because Robin is a horticulturalist, I assumed she would know both the common and the Latin name of this rose—but no luck. Years earlier, a Vermont gardening friend of mine thought that the rose might be Father Hugo. Robin disagreed. Besides: how could *Alice's* rose sport a man's name? Though it looks similar, our rose has flatter petals than Father Hugo. So we both call her Alice's Rose.

Henrietta, who lived next door in Watertown, was fastidious about her yard. When we first moved into our new house, we noticed her bent over the sidewalk, sweeping up tiny bits of debris with a small broom and dustpan. To our horror, we soon learned that she didn't appreciate Alice's rose. We went on a brief vacation, when the rose was covered with tiny buds, and returned to find it chopped to the ground. An expensive climber from White Flower Farm—a gift from my mother-in-law—also lay scattered in pieces across our small driveway.

I was appalled. I told our friend and fellow gardener, Randy Hesse, about this assault. (Randy's garden boasts an impressive version of Alice's rose.) "What would you suggest?" I asked.

His laugh was grim. "Have you considered a small bomb?"

This was a defining moment. I could either start a border war, or find a way to get along. As if Alice, with her years of anti-war activities, had whispered in my ear, I knocked on Henrietta's door. At first, she denied having cut the roses, then suddenly announced, in her fierce, Irish accent, "They were touching MOY fence."

I took a deep breath. "I'm sorry," I said. "Next time you're upset about something in our yard, please let me know, and I'll prune it. And feel free to cut some roses for yourself, when it blooms again."

Henrietta never said another word about our yard. In later years, she even praised our flowering shrubs and perennials. I moved the climber and was careful to prune Alice so that she didn't touch the fence. For its part, the rose behaved as if that early slashing were normal. It shot back up and was soon over six feet tall. Each spring, its fragile blooms covered the canes like a delicate ball gown. Henrietta didn't complain. Perhaps she realized she could enjoy the blossoms without the bother of caring for the plant.

Ten years later, the rose was out of control. After its annual flowering, I hauled our tallest stepladder from the basement to lop off the topmost branches. A metal door slammed and Henrietta appeared, carrying her own clippers. "Like some help?" she asked.

I accepted happily. The rose was a peacemaker. Alice Holway—long gone to the Great Garden in the Sky—would be smiling.

Part Four
Gardens and Memory

If ever we see those gardens again,
The summer will be gone—at least our summer.
Some other mockingbird will concertize
Among the mulberries, and other vines
Will climb the high brick wall to disappear.
—Dana Gioia
The Lost Garden

When a garden is gone,
the land remembers.
—Phyllis Root

Highbush Cranberry

Viburnum trilobum

How did I write an entire book
about the gardens in my life—yet omit the camp, the little Vermont
cottage whose gardens I loved more than any other? Why has the camp
been invisible, in this memoir?

Four years after John and I purchased The Birdhouse with its Last
Garden, we had to tear the camp down. Sadly, the bulldozer also tore
through the gardens that surrounded it. As my friend Jackie Briggs Martin
said, "The story disappeared because the gardens were gone." To write

about the camp is to experience the pain of losing it all over again. Yet those gardens—and the memories they evoke—deserve their own story.

The camp, as my parents called it, was a small yellow house at the end of Kirby Hollow Road in Dorset. Perched on a rectangular piece of flat land, the house overlooked a cow pasture. A low crooked gate opened into the sloping field, and a nearby vernal pool nourished salamanders, frogs and spring peepers.

The view from the house was spectacular. From an altitude of about 1700 feet, we looked out across the Mettawee River valley to stately Mother Myrick, with Mount Equinox in the distance. A mile from the nearest neighbor and far from any city lights, the sky shimmered with stars. On cold winter nights, the Milky Way spread across the sky in a carpet of glittering, winking jewels.

The house itself was a hodge-podge, created when earlier owners moved an icehouse and a chicken house from a farm in the valley, mashing them together to create a cabin with a single tiny bedroom and bath. The kitchen, dining area and living room were all one space. When my parents bought Saddleback Farm, the tiny house was in bad shape. They renovated the kitchen, added a bigger bedroom with a plate-glass window that looked out on the view, and called it their camp. They lived there for a year, while local carpenters constructed their future home in the valley below. My father then used the camp as an office for another year. A photo from that era shows my mother and a friend standing in what would eventually become the yard, surrounded by curious, unfenced Polled Hereford cows.

During the camp's early years, we had picnics in the yard when cousins visited in the summer. On one memorable summer evening, the Ketchum and Ransom families (friends in both Bronxville and Dorset) picnicked together. Gail Ransom and I were both very pregnant, and we laughed as we rested paper plates, heavy with sweet corn, on our round bellies.

My parents then rented the camp to Dan and Cindy O'Leary, who raised their two daughters in that small, cozy space. A mile from the nearest neighbor, the rough road could be treacherous in winter and impassable in mud season. Once or twice, it was washed out entirely by floods. Yet the O'Learys loved the little house and stayed until they could build their own place in the valley. Then a series of tenants moved in and out of the camp. The last renters trashed the house and didn't pay the rent. When Dad evicted them, he found the plate-glass window cracked, the walls coated in a film of cigarette smoke, and grime everywhere.

Though John and I had just purchased our house in Watertown, we begged Dad not to rent it out again. "It's a mess," Dad warned, but we didn't care. Living in the city, we longed for quiet and access to nature. Derek came down from Burlington to help us clean. Ethan spent a long weekend with us, painting the walls. We scrubbed, vacuumed and scoured yard sales for furniture and kitchen supplies.

And I took on the gardens. Though choked with weeds, there were actually some narrow, stony flowerbeds next to the house. A previous, short-term tenant had worked at a nursery; she had planted a few perennials before moving on. As I dug into the tangles, I found iris, a clump of day lilies (which turned out to be a warm, sunny yellow, rather than the ubiquitous orange), and a few hostas. We took over the house in the summer, so it wasn't until the following spring, after arriving late one night, that we woke to a deafening chorus of spring peepers and the sight of daffodils opening in sunny spots around the yard.

A bowl of mountains above the camp (called "The Devil's Armchair" by old-timers, due to its encircling shape), creates the steep watershed filling the brook that eventually drains into the Mettawee River. Sleeping in the camp's magical bedroom, with its view of the mountains, was blissful. Except in winter, when the brook froze into silence, the rush of water lulled us to sleep with its natural white noise. A deep spring above the camp created a gravity-fed water source for the house. The spring never ran dry, even in summers of drought.

Eight hundred acres of woodland, adjacent to national forest land, surrounded the camp, so wildlife was plentiful. In the summer, the *harunk-harunk* of frogs in the vernal pool sang a steady chorus. Redwing blackbirds nested in the shrubs that leaned over the pool, swallows wheeled above the yard, catching flies, and an occasional bluebird flashed in the cattails. Redtail hawks sailed the thermals above the pasture, and a phoebe built her nest on the eaves of the house every year.

One fall evening we arrived at dusk. I walked out to the edge of the yard to pick an apple from the old tree and nearly stepped in a steaming pile of bear manure. (I clapped my hands to announce our arrival, in case the bear was still nearby.) Coyotes often yipped and howled in the meadow at night, while the barred owl hooted: "Who cooks for you-awlll?"

In addition to these critters, we also had moose. John and I were walking down the road toward the brook one morning when we spotted a moose trotting down the log road to our left. She stopped; we stopped. We didn't move for a long time, neither did she: a game of chicken. Did she have a calf? If so, we didn't dare spook her. She probably wished we'd leave, so that she could drink from the cold pool below the culvert. Before we took the first step, she turned and lumbered back up the hill, disappearing into the forest.

For sixteen years, John and I drove up to the camp on weekends and took extended vacations there in the summer. In good weather, I spent most of every weekend in the gardens. I transplanted peonies and iris from our city garden. Friends divided plants and gave me the extras, or brought perennials as gifts when they visited. John and I devoted a few weekends to creating a border for peonies under the bedroom window, replacing stones and broken glass with rich compost. I planted Rocky Mountain Columbine in honor of Ali, our Colorado daughter-in-law; Virginia bluebells for my aunt Janet; and a lilac—because every Vermont house needs a lilac, even though the shrub is not native and doesn't host local birds or insects. And of course I transplanted two cuttings of Alice's rose, one on each side of the bathroom window. The rose was happier there than in any other garden I've created.

In spite of the altitude and the cold winters, flowers and shrubs thrived at the camp. Was it the sweet soil? The fact that frost drains into the valley, so my parents' house, 500 feet below us, suffered frost when we didn't? Was it the compost we fed the plants? Or the snow that piled up over the beds in winter, providing natural insulation? Maybe all of the above. But I like to think that our new love nurtured the gardens, as did the feeling that we were building a home for my sons to enjoy with us. Derek and Ali spent one spring and summer at the camp, building fences for the cows; they were married on the crest of the cow pasture just beyond the pond. The guests sat on hay bales as they spoke their vows, beneath a birch bower their friends had made. During that summer, Ali broke sod and created a small vegetable and herb garden beside the fence. Ethan brought Vermont friends to stay and celebrate art openings and holidays. We had at least one cozy Christmas there, with six of us squeezed into the three small rooms.

Living at the camp could be an adventure. One memorable winter, when my parents were still alive, our car slid off the road in a snowstorm after Christmas dinner at their house. John and I abandoned the car and climbed the hill in our boots and holiday finery. Snowflakes sizzled on the roasting pan with its leftover chicken as we found our way up in the dark.

When friends visited, they had to tolerate the tiny guest room and the shared bath. Sarah Stone, a colleague of John's and a close friend, was especially enthusiastic about the camp. She and her husband visited us there one stunning October weekend. We all hiked up the steep hill to the Saddle Meadows. The following September, Sarah brought chicken and prunes, ingredients for a traditional Rosh Hashanah dish. When she died—much too young—of ovarian cancer, we planted a highbush cranberry in her memory, next to the pond. Sarah loved birds, and we knew that redwing blackbirds, nesting near the pond, would enjoy its berries. The bush thrived, and we enjoyed watching the birds fly in and out of the foliage, showing their quick flashes of red.

My parents loved the camp as much as we did. When they died, we hosted a family lunch in the yard on a fresh June morning, after their burial in the Dorset cemetery. In an echo of that long-ago family picnic—when Gail Ransom and I were pregnant with our first babies—Ali and Vita were both expecting that summer. Just turned three, our older grandkids crouched in the squishy mud beside the pond, trying to catch frogs.

But the camp idyll didn't last. The town stopped plowing the road, and refused to maintain it, even in the summer. We fought—and lost—a court battle to keep the road open. Without a basement, and built on wet clay, the house grew moldy, triggering allergies; a minor earthquake cracked the foundation. As the road deteriorated, we risked being stranded without access to fire or rescue trucks—and the gas company was reluctant to send their truck up the narrow hill. (Who could blame them?) Besides, we were getting older. Living a mile from the nearest neighbor, at the end of a long, steep road, seemed foolish. We started to think about other options. When The Birdhouse came on the market, we pounced on it.

Over the next two years, we cleaned out the camp and I slowly moved perennials (peonies, iris, hostas and herbs) down the hill to The Birdhouse gardens. Most shrubs—such as the lilac, Sarah's cranberry and Alice's rose—were too big to move. When we finally decided to tear the house down, everything happened fast—too fast! Because an excavator and dump truck were already at The Birdhouse, finishing site work on our renovation, their trucks churned up the hill unexpectedly, engines grinding. Demolition began before I was ready—but maybe I never would be.

I made the mistake of hiking up the hill to watch on the second day of the teardown. We had hoped to move the myrtle that John had so carefully trained to surround the outdoor shower; I wanted to transplant the clump of sunshine-yellow daylilies—but we were too late. The house was already gone. Dust swirled above a heap of rotten boards, broken glass, firebricks, and copper pipe, as two men loaded the debris into a dump truck. There was no sign that people had gardened—much less lived—on that site.

Dust caught in my lungs and I had a fit of coughing that reminded me, bitterly, of the pneumonia I'd developed the last time I'd been inside the house; it was, after all, a sick building. I turned and stumbled down the rutted driveway, blinded by tears. Memories scrolled past like a sped-up movie: the hours spent digging and weeding; the labor of covering plants against deep frost; the joy of seeing green shoots poke through straw the next spring; the smell of the lilac when I gathered the blooms and cradled them against my chest; the battle-scar scratches along my arms from pruning Alice's rose. I remembered late fall days, when hunters stalked the woods for deer while John and I—wearing neon orange vests—wrestled our homemade wooden shelters over the holly bushes. Our fingers grew numb as we stapled burlap across the wood to protect the shrubs from winter burn. The holly finally grew tall enough, as we had hoped, to shield the gas tank.

Now it was gone. All of it. Gone.

A few weeks after the demolition, we hiked up the road, this time with Derek, Ali and their girls. We scattered wildflower seeds on the rough, leveled ground. The view was still there, of course, beyond the crooked gate. Derek and Ali held hands, perhaps remembering the months they lived there; the preparation for their wedding in the pasture, where cows now cropped the rough brush and grass beyond the fence. A Siberian iris bloomed by the pond, and frogs hopped from the banks as we approached. Redwing blackbirds flew in and out of Sarah's highbush cranberry as they had for years, snapping up fruit while a swallow swooped in for bugs.

Decades from now, will hikers come up the old rutted road, walk out onto this flat ground where the house once stood—and wonder about its past? Will they hear frogs harrumphing in the pond, listen to the hum of the brook, and wonder who lived here? If they come in the spring, will the daffodils still bloom, hinting that someone once loved and gardened here, with the gray-blue mountains of Mother Myrick and Equinox in the distance? I will look for lilac shoots next spring, and perhaps the wildflower seeds we scattered will come up. But the gardens live on only in memory.

I hope that Phyllis is right—that the land remembers it all: the squeals of toddlers racing across the grass; the laughter of friends sharing a beer as smoke from the barbecue twists to the sky; and the happiness of our early days here, when we were first married, creating the gardens we tended with love.

The garden's heart, the lilies
in consoling perfumes, the richesse of memory.
—Gail Mazur
At Land's End

Daylily

Hemerocallis

Three years after we buy The Birdhouse, we undertake a major renovation that lasts a full year. A new wing includes a downstairs bedroom with an alcove whose windows look out on a stone wall, built by our neighbor, Paul Ferenc, using stones gathered on the property. An ancient, stately maple casts shade across the wall. We can sit on a comfy loveseat, inside the alcove, and look up to the Saddle.

I turn seventy just before the renovation is finished, during a June as beautiful as any in my memory. The peonies at The Birdhouse are lush, many of the perennials that I moved from the camp (such as iris and baptesia) are well established, while those I planted for pollinators are attracting honeybees, native bees, swallowtail and monarch butterflies—just as we hoped.

One weekend I pick up Sydney Eddison's practical book, *Gardening for a Lifetime: How to Garden Wiser as You Grow Older*. I sit on the love seat in our new bedroom, reading. Full of smart suggestions, the book lists ways to save on back-breaking labor, cut back on chores, and simplify. So why, as I enter a new decade with diminished energy, weak legs, and arthritis in my hands, are we creating a daylily garden outside the alcove windows?

Because that patch of ground, beneath the maple, is at eye height when we sit in our bedroom alcove. The area demands something more interesting than weeds—though of course, a bed of native ferns or simple ground cover would suffice. But Vermont, aptly known as the Green Mountain State, is relentlessly green in the summer. I decide to plant lilies for color, and in memory of our dear friend, Ellen Levine, who died just before we bought The Birdhouse.

For many years, Ellen and her partner, Anne Koedt, lived on the other side of the mountain that divides our area of Vermont from New York State. Ellen and Anne spent one backbreaking summer digging a daylily bed, and during that time, they introduced us to Slate Hill Farm, owned by a couple who raise and propagate daylilies. Spread out below the side of the eponymous hill, a few acres of lilies bloom in a riot of color that evokes the Biblical "lilies of the field." We love to trek over the mountain, walk among the blooms, and choose lilies with names such as "The Pride of Massachusetts" (a bright lemon yellow), or "Hook and Ladder" (a dazzling red). When The Birdhouse renovations are done, I decide to plant another half dozen lilies among the roots of the maple, hoping they will provide color and beauty next year.

Daylilies are native to Asia, not New England, so they go against my desire for native plants. I do see bees foraging in their deep cups, but lilies are not even listed in the index of Tallamy's book, *Bringing Nature Home*. Still: Ellen loved them, and we miss her terribly. Planting them brings her back, at least in memory.

John and I have reached the phase of life where we deal constantly with loss. The list of friends and family who have died, in the past ten years or more, is long. With each passing, we tend to plant a tree, or a shrub, or some flower that evokes that person in our memory, as we did for Sarah Stone at the camp. For my father, we planted a white oak at the end of The Birdhouse yard; for my mother, who loved fall colors, I buy rusty orange mums in September and dig them in beside my parents' grave. And for my murdered college roommate, Turid Sato, we planted a flowering crabapple surrounded by tulips, in our city garden.

In Turid's case, the joke was on us. Turid was a flashy dresser who loved bright colors. The first fall, we planted yellow tulips. They came up red, with ruffled petals. I assumed the bin had been mislabeled or that I'd grabbed the wrong ones. So I was careful, the next fall, to order yellow daffodils from a catalog. This batch came up orange with red stripes. In a third year, the tulips were the right color, but doubled, with frilly, fringed petals. Was she teasing us from beyond the grave?

A few years ago, our dear friends Jock and Lorni lost their young son Matt, killed in an accident that left us all with broken hearts. In the saddest memorial of all, we planted what we *thought* was a young walnut tree—which a friend had started from a single walnut—in Matt's memory. Once small enough to travel in a bucket, the tree took off, gaining in height every year until I couldn't reach its top branches.

But this past summer, something was off. Should walnut branches feel sticky? Walnut wood is famously hard and strong. Why were its branches breaking so easily when squirrels jumped into it from the nearby lilac bush? I pulled out my tree guide and studied the leaves. They were compound and seemed to match the picture of the walnut leaves in the book—maybe. The next day, I spotted a tree that looked similar, growing like a weed (uh-oh), in a scraggly clump of brush on my brother's driveway. I broke off a branch and brought it home. It matched the leaves on our tree—as well as the picture of a staghorn sumac in my tree guide. Walnut and sumac are on adjoining pages in the book—perhaps because their leaves are similar?

But: a lowly sumac! At first, I was devastated. Digging the hole had been arduous; Ethan spent hours wrestling a big pile of stones from the ground to make room for the tree's roots. We had fenced it to keep the deer away, fed it fresh compost each fall, marveled at how fast it grew. We imagined our grandchildren gathering the walnuts in some distant future. Matt was sturdy and strong, as I imagined the mature tree would be. Plus, my friend Claire had tended the seedling with loving care and imagined it growing in our yard. Had we done all this for a silly weed?

Then I had to laugh. Matt was known for his wicked sense of humor. I could easily imagine him chortling if I had told him the story. "At least I didn't give you a *poison* sumac," he might say, ribbing us.

Earlier in the spring, before we realized our mistake, we planted a hazelnut tree, grown by the state's Department of Natural Resources. We planted it on the small hill, visible from our bedroom window. I've heard that hazelnuts grow fast, and our small specimen even came with an identifying tag. We'd been faithfully watering the sapling since its spring planting, and it has put out some fresh leaves. We decided that Matt now has a new tree.

Memorializing our loved ones this way may seem morbid to some, and of course our plantings can't bring anyone back or banish our grief. A crabapple tree couldn't mimic Turid's brilliant mind and infectious laugh. A highbush cranberry attracts the birds but doesn't evoke Sarah's compassion, her love of life. A daylily is fluttery and bends easily in the wind, no match for Ellen's savvy or her rabble-rousing, lifelong quest for justice. While no tree planted in Matt's honor could match his unique view of life, now he and Ellen are side by side in a patch of our yard. Watch out, world!

A daylily is ephemeral—hence its name. But so is our time on earth. As Stanley Kunitz wrote in his final book (published just after he turned 100): life and death are intertwined in the garden. That is deeply comforting for those of us who are left behind.

Part of the fascination of gardening is that it is, on the one hand,
a practical exercise of the human body and, on the other,
a direct participation in the ritual of life and death.
—Stanley Kunitz
The Wild Braid

Black Oak

Quercus velutina

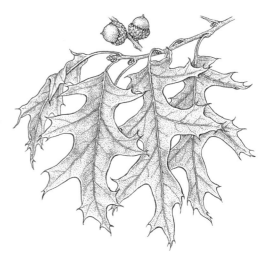

In the summer of 2004, I asked my parents if I could raise flowers in their back yard, for Derek and Ali's wedding. For decades, Mom and Dad had gardened in an enormous vegetable plot near their barn, giving them easy access to manure from their farm animals. As they aged, that plot became too big to manage, so they created a smaller garden close to their house. Now, during the spring before the wedding, they faced physical challenges that made gardening difficult. They were spending more time in their retirement community in northern Vermont, and their small veggie plot was full of weeds. So they were delighted with my idea.

I arrived in May to prepare the soil for planting. Black flies and mosquitoes swarmed as I forked up the heavy black earth and yanked out weeds and crabgrass. I swatted at the bugs as I turned the soil. The steady *rap-tap* of Dad's cane sounded from the slate walk and I was glad for the interruption. He entered the garden, reached into his pocket and, with no preamble, held out his cupped fist.

"Open your hands," he said.

Puzzled, I pulled off my gloves and obeyed. Dad tipped a clutch of acorns into my palms. "From the black oak in the village. I gathered them last fall, kept them in the fridge over the winter." His brown eyes—one cloudy, the other clear, like *his* father's at the same age—fixed on mine. "Plant them for me, will you?"

That was it: no further instructions. Dad stumped away. I wiped my hands on my jeans and cupped the acorns. Smooth and dry, their pointed tips were sharp against my skin. Though it's a well-worn cliché, it still seems astonishing, even miraculous, that an enormous oak—symbol of wisdom, with its craggy bark and wide, spreading branches—could develop from such a small seed.

I set the acorns on the wall, laid out a row with stakes and string as Dad had always done in his own gardens, and hoed a trench. As I placed the acorns in the soil, I couldn't help thinking that my father, now in his eighties, must know his years were numbered. He might never see the trees that would struggle to take root in the cold, spring soil. Yet ever the visionary, he imagined the sturdy seedlings reaching for the sun.

I forgot about the acorns as the summer went on. Raising the wedding flowers turned out to be a challenging adventure. A woodchuck tunneled under the wall and helped himself to the tasty flower seedlings as they emerged. I covered the remaining seedlings with a light-weight row cover and anchored the fabric to the ground to keep the tiny sprouts safe. We had too little rain early in the summer; too much as the wedding date approached. Some sunflowers tipped over in a storm and needed staking; the zinnias blossomed later than we had hoped.

Somehow, enough flowers survived. The day before the wedding, my childhood friend Sally arrived to help. (We had each been maid or matron of honor at each other's first weddings, so it was fitting for us to do this together.) We cut a mix of dahlias, cosmos, nicotiana, sunflowers and zinnias as a steady rain fell. We soaked the flowers overnight in buckets filled with a mix of bleach, water and lemon juice, suggested by my friend Chuck, a florist.

The next morning, family members and friends picked wildflowers from nearby meadows and we all arranged the bouquets in mason jars. My artistic aunt Janet cut flowering branches from the oakleaf hydrangea and created a huge arrangement for the tent's banquet table. We balanced sunflowers in metal sap buckets and set them on either side of the wedding bower that the couple's friends had made from birch saplings. The weather cleared; a crisp break between storms. We sat on hay bales as Derek and Ali spoke their vows against the backdrop of the mountains. A perfect day.

When I returned to the garden after the wedding to clean up stakes, cloth and wire hoops, I realized that Dad's acorns had never sprouted. The string sagged over the row where I'd covered them in May. I weeded carefully, in case I'd missed a seedling, but didn't find anything. By then, our parents had returned to their retirement community. Dad never asked about the acorns. Had he forgotten? Did the acorns fail to sprout because he hadn't followed the complex instructions about wintering them over? (Doubtful: Dad was meticulous *and* a perfectionist.) Did I bury them too deep? Did the woodchuck eat the seedlings before they had a chance to grow? Had I not given them proper attention?

Now both parents are gone, buried side by side in the Dorset cemetery. A two hundred-year-old oak guards the cemetery entrance. The oak's gnarled branches, thick as any tree trunk, twist and turn toward the sky. In the fall, a carpet of acorns covers the ground at its feet. A local conservation organization, knowing our parents' love of trees, created a

Memorial Tree Fund in their memory, dedicated to the care, pruning and feeding of this giant oak.

Dad would be honored, though embarrassed, by the attention.

Oak is a keystone species. When building a stone arch, a keystone is the central stone that holds the structure together. If the keystone fails, the arch collapses. In the same way, oaks play an essential part in a forest's ecosystem. In the northern woodlands that I know best, animals as diverse as bears, turkeys, squirrels, blue jays and quail rely on acorns for food. An oak's wide-reaching limbs create shade as well as shelter for small birds and raptors. Over the centuries, native people gathered acorns and processed them for soup, gruel and hot cakes. When an oak dies, its death touches everything else in the forest.

Oak trees remind me of my father. He was a big man, well over six feet. I remember standing at his knee as a child, craning my neck to see his head. He seemed as tall as any tree and sometimes as unyielding. He was also intensely private, like an oak whose craggy bark protects its inner secrets.

When an ancient oak falls, the ground shakes under the force of its weight. The loss of its spreading limbs leaves a gaping hole in the forest canopy. Dad's death affected our family in the same way.

And so, on our second summer at The Birdhouse, John and I planted an oak in Dad's memory. Not a black oak, but the white *Quercus alba.* According to Edward Tallamy, author of *Bringing Nature Home,* white oaks do more than feed woodland animals. They also host as many as 400 species of insects, butterflies, and birds. Now, when I drive past the cemetery oak, or water our own young tree, I remember the touch of my father's fingers as he dropped the acorns into my palms. They were seeds of the future, gathered in the village he loved—a future he wouldn't live to see.

The most charitable thing to be said about November weather
is that it is sure to be uncertain. The sere autumn leaves rattle
disconcertingly underfoot, each gust of wind brings the taste
and smell of winter... The first snow flurries are not far off,
and one day when we least expect them they will slant in unannounced...
—Richard M. Ketchum
Second Cutting

Christmas Rose

Genus: Rosa

When my parents first moved
to their retirement home, on the
shores of Lake Champlain, they
lived in a cottage with its own
garden, where they grew many of their favorite perennials. As their
health failed, they moved into the Residential Care building. They missed
their private garden but enjoyed spending time in the facility's lovely
fenced garden that they dubbed "The Secret Garden," after the novel we
all loved.

After a resident died in this community (an event that happens too often at an end-of-life facility), the staff placed a single red rose in a bud vase on a table in the entryway of the main building. A small card, propped against the vase, announced the name of the resident who had passed away.

The sight of these red roses sent a shiver through the residents whenever the staff placed one on the table. Soon, my parents and I agreed that we never wanted to see a red rose again. When I sent them cut flowers—which I often did in the winter months—I always instructed the florist *not* to include red roses.

Our parents died quickly, one right after the other. First my mom went, and a red rose in her memory stood on the skilled nursing desk as well as in the main lobby. Dad died exactly twelve weeks later, to the day. We were devastated, but not surprised. As Dad loved to tell us, he first spotted Mom on the other side of a dance floor when he was fifteen and she was a year older. He asked his friend who she was. "That's Barbara Bray," his friend replied. "Why?"

"Because I'm going to marry her," Dad told him.

When his beloved "Bobs" passed away, they'd known each other for more than seventy years. He couldn't go on without her. So red roses appeared on the tables again.

Valentine's Day arrived a month after Dad's death. Bouquets of red roses, bundled in the windows of every florist in town, made me weep. I avoided the flower section at the supermarket for months.

That fall, Superstorm Sandy barreled into town, the thousand-mile storm that shredded the fabric of so many shoreline communities in New York and New Jersey. In Massachusetts, we had heavy winds and rain, but escaped true devastation when the storm veered away from the coast. Then an early November snow, wet and heavy, blanketed the ground. The cold snap blackened the last of our dahlias (already smashed by the wind) and flattened the chives and parsley in our city garden. As I cleared my windshield the next morning, a spot of red caught my eye. I clomped through the wet snow to the back yard. A single red rose had opened against the wooden fence. I went inside for my clippers. Gently, I shook snow from the petals, brought the rose inside, and set it in a bud vase. Like Dad's Christmas Rose so many years ago, it had refused to succumb to the weather.

The storms had arrived close to the first anniversary of my mom's death. I remembered that on the day of her memorial service, I had glanced out the window to see thick snowflakes drifting down, though it was October. It also snowed on my dad's memorial, three months later. Now, this November rose seemed like a message from our parents, especially from Dad: "Remember the Christmas Rose."

Part Five
Gardens and the Wheel of Life

To garden is to elide past, present and future; it is a defiance of time.
You garden today for tomorrow; the garden mutates from season to season,
always the same but always different...
And gardening, in its small way, performs a memory feat: it corrals time,
pinning it to the seasons, to the gardening year, by summoning up the garden
in the past, the garden to come. A garden is never just now;
it suggests yesterday and tomorrow; it does not allow time its steady progress.
—Penelope Lively
Life in the Garden

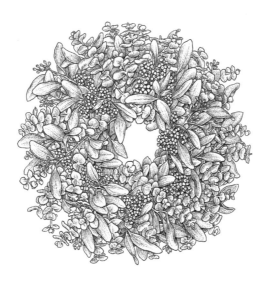

I am one of those unfortunates who when they lose something they love can't immediately replace it with a new model.
—Eleanor Perényi
Green Thoughts: A writer in the Garden

Blazing Star

Liatris spicata

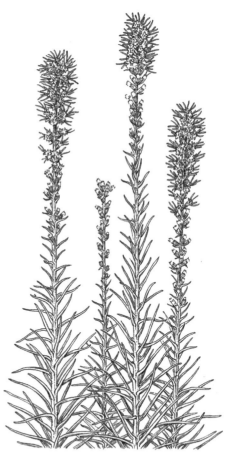

A week after a wrenching, exhausting move into a condo, John and I drive back to our tall, skinny house in the city—labeled "The Blue House" by our grandkids—where we lived for twenty-one years. The house is now under contract and the new owners will take possession in a few days. We have left the urban oasis that we created over two decades. Now our city garden will consist of planters perched on a narrow balcony.

Granted, our new unit has a fabulous view of Boston, with a southeast exposure on one side, and lovely afternoon light on the other. House plants will thrive there, and when I first peered over the wall separating our balcony from our neighbors, I noticed that they were growing chives, parsley and other herbs among bright annuals: a colorful display. There's hope for a different kind of garden, and we are moving on.

We park in front of our old house and unload a random collection of pails and buckets. John disappears down the bulkhead stairs to fetch the lone shovel we saved for this night, while I admire the garden one last time. As if to taunt us—or perhaps to remind us of the literal blood, sweat and tears that marked the physical effort of building this garden from scratch—the garden has never been so lush and abundant. In spite of a dangerously dry June, every perennial, shrub and tree has outdone itself.

The drama began in April, when the Zumi crabapple exploded in curtains of blossoms. Our realtor sent his photographer over to capture its beauty for the agency's promotional flier. In May, the peony blooms were so heavy that the hoops bent under their weight. Now, the pollinator garden is behaving just as I intended when I dug the first spindly plants into the ground: it is alive with honey bees, bumble bees and occasional butterflies. I've even seen a monarch recently. And one final miracle: after twenty years of failure, a lavender plant actually survived the winter. Its flowers spill out over my feet from the raised bed, the scent wafting toward me in the dusk. Is its success due to heat from climate change, or better care? Probably both.

Bands of black-eyed Susans nod along the fence, while daisies—a gift from my gardening friend Fran just a year before—have expanded to fill the spot where the grandkids and I once grew pumpkins. Fuchsia pink bee balm lives up to its name: bumble bees of every shape and size flit in and out of its blossoms. They quiver over the blue agastache, the purple coneflowers, and the sturdy liatris (also called blazing star). Liatris was new to me when I planted it last spring. Deep purple blossoms, shaped like bottle brushes, top its grassy stems. It already looks well established.

But we aren't here to admire—rather, to steal. Of course, we still own the property, so technically, we can take what we want. Besides, the new owners told us, in the note that came with their offer, that they might grow more vegetables and fewer flowers. We're happy that they care about the garden, but there are a few select plants that I can't abandon. John emerges with the shovel, I gather the buckets and tubs we brought for this purpose, and we start to dig.

First: the agastache. The realtor jammed the "House For Sale" sign up against its fuzzy stem. Time to liberate the plant? We wrestle its roots from their imprisonment and cover them with loose soil in a bucket. Next we gently scoop the butterfly weed from its precarious spot in the raised bed where I grow herbs and early lettuce. It hurts to leave the glorious lavender, but it would never survive a Vermont winter. We have plenty of purple coneflowers at The Birdhouse, but I can always find room for an extra clump of Joe Pye weed. John's shovel clangs against the hard-packed dry ground as he splits off a few stalks. I cup my hands under the roots, scoop up a bit of soil for coverage, and set the transplants into an old flowerpot.

Last, but not least, John carves a circle under the liatris with the shovel's sharp blade. Its roots are deep and tangled among the spreading roots of the inkberry bushes that have hidden the ugly chain link fence for years. It's a delicate job to separate them. Together we lift the liatris from the hole and set it in a big tub. We water the roots and lug the tub to the car, wedging it and the other plants between small pieces of furniture and odds and ends from the move.

The garden seems to glow in the dusk. John fills in the holes and I smooth them over with my hands. ("Hiding the evidence?" our dear friend and neighbor Elana teases me later.)

I stand in the driveway for one long moment while memories wash over. I remember the early days, when every pass of the shovel clanged against broken glass, bricks or rebar; the hours that John and our young friend Michael spent lugging railroad ties and stone to create raised beds and a small terrace around the smaller crabapple. I remember how Robin visited and imagined a garden where I could only see debris; how she sketched out the plan that we followed (and revised) that transformed the property.

I think of starting pumpkins with the grandkids, following the cycle from seed to jack-o-lantern; and I remember showing two little boys, both born on this alley, how to plant lettuce and beans.

I also remember the winter known as "Snowmaggeden," when it snowed almost every day, leading to record-breaking snowfalls, with a final tally of 110 inches. Seven *feet* of snow buried these gardens, the piles of shoveled snow were 8-10 feet high; even our tallest shrubs disappeared. Yet somehow, the garden survived; tulip and daffodils emerged late, but sturdy; the reddish first buds of the peonies poked through the saturated soil as if nothing unusual had happened.

I take one last walk along our narrow paths now, bidding farewell to the crabapple we planted in Turid's memory, the spring after she was murdered. I brush a hand over the kerria that our friend Nancy gave us before she died—much too suddenly—of heart disease. It needs to be pruned, but that's not my worry now. I whisper goodbye to the peonies, which traveled from Vermont to Boston, so many years ago, changing color along the way (from pink to white) yet never losing their vigor. Nothing will ever be as painful as leaving the house where I raised my sons, yet this farewell triggers the Vermont memories I thought I had buried. As if my divorce were yesterday, rather than decades ago, I swipe at my tears with a muddy glove, climb into the car, and take one last look as we back down the alley.

When we first moved in, no one on the street had a garden. Now, all three houses boast flowering shrubs and perennials—including some I divided and shared with the neighbors: yellow and purple iris, hostas, lady's mantle and coneflowers. The garden will live on through our friends, no matter what the new owners decide to do.

The transplants sit in the condo garage all night, and I worry: Will they stay cool? Did I give them enough water? We drive north early the next morning. The car is fragrant with blossoms, damp foliage and wet soil. When we reach The Birdhouse, we haul the pots into the shade. I turn on the hose. The agastache is already humming with bees—even though it still sits in its clay pot. A bumble bee hovers beside the tallest spiky stem of the liatris. The word is already out.

Ten days later, our D.C. granddaughters visit us at The Birdhouse. In an echo of the past, when I cut flowers with my own grandmother, the girls help me choose flowers for fresh table bouquets. The transplants are all doing well—except for the butterfly weed, which looks dead. I knew it was a prairie plant, and out of its element. Plus, Robin had warned me that butterfly weed hates to be moved. (Who could blame it? I hate moving, too.) However, closer inspection a day later shows one tiny whorl of green on a sad stalk—so I keep watering, just in case. We've had a lot of rain, so the agastache and liatris are thriving, healthy enough to cut for table arrangements. The girls and I are careful not to disturb the bees that are hard at work this early in the morning. If these transplants are anything like me, they'll be happier in Vermont than in the city, where they will have deep soil, plenty of rain most years, and a wealth of pollinators, including hummingbirds, monarchs, and, just the other day, a vivid swallowtail butterfly.

As the girls and I circulate around the yard, choosing flowers for their color and size, I realize that this garden now holds pieces of every garden I've ever created, in city or country. It's also a testament to all the gardeners—friends and family members—who shared plants and gardening secrets with me, as well as the wise gardeners whose books have been my constant companions along the way. It's a garden of the past, the present, and the future.

One may progress through life surrounded on all sides by drabness,
but if there are butterflies at the center,
there will never be a want of beauty or romance.
—Anne Fadiman
At Large and At Small

Joe Pye Weed

Eutrochium maculatum

One August afternoon, two weeks after we have liberated those few perennials from our city garden and said farewell to our little alley, I head out to The Birdhouse garden, colander in hand, to pick pole beans. The large clump of Joe Pye weed—which has exploded from a single spindly plant of a few years ago—is in full bloom, its frothy, pale lavender flowers waving in a slight breeze. As I approach, a flicker of orange winks in the sunshine, then another.

Monarchs!

I set the colander down and inch closer, holding my breath, but butterflies flit around me, unconcerned, touching down on one blossom, then another; rising and falling as if checking out which flower offers the sweetest flavor. I count: nine monarchs. *Nine.* They sip each flower in preparation for their long flight south, like marathoners bulking up on carbs before the race. I stand transfixed for a long time, then slip into the house to beckon John out. We tiptoe into the flowerbed, but the monarchs ignore us as we watch for a long time, hardly daring to breathe. Then, one by one, the butterflies flicker away, sunlight winking on their wings. My eyes blur with tears. I'm transported by delight—and gratitude—as we bid them goodbye. "Good luck," I whisper, assuming they are off on their journey.

But they reappear the next afternoon, as if they had promised each other: *Meet at The Birdhouse garden, same time*. Again, there are nine. (The *same* nine?). On the third afternoon, they visit again, at four o'clock. On the fourth day, only three show up. The next day: none.

When I was young, monarchs were as ubiquitous as fireflies, beautiful and beloved, yet so common we took them for granted. In recent summers, monarchs have appeared only occasionally, one or two at most, at a time. The winking of fireflies, at dusk, has been just as rare. But now: a *flock* of monarchs!

After they depart, I realize I know nothing about the origin of the Joe Pye weed that drew them to our garden. Who—or what—was Joe Pye? A cursory search attributes the name to a Mohican healer, who might have used the plant to cure fever. (Some historical accounts say he was active in the 17th century, while others claim he was treating people as late as the 1800s.) Legends also report that early colonists grew Joe Pye weed as a cure for typhus, kidney stones and urinary tract infections. But a deeper search leads me to a long, scientific treatise and exploration of the legend, with some historians giving credit to a Joseph Shauquethqueat, who called the plant Seneca Snakeroot. He may have moved west out of New England after colonists seized his ancestral lands. The authors of this paper couldn't come to a definite conclusion about the source of the name, though they surmise that Joe—or Joseph—was a real person. Whether or not Joe Pye weed was a healing plant then, it clearly sustains these monarchs now.

When we began to garden with bees in mind, I purchased a sign announcing that our yard was a "Honeybee Haven." However, we don't raise honeybees, and native bees are even more essential to the pollination of important food crops. For that reason, I ordered a sign from the Xerces Society. It tells anyone passing by that our yard is a "Pollinator Habitat," protecting all types of pollinators (from bees to birds to butterflies) from exposure to pesticides.

Gardening with a focus on pollinators brings rewards in all seasons. It is a pleasure to wander into the garden and find four different types of bees humming and buzzing on the abundant purple stalks of my anise hyssop. (Little did I know, in the past, how many different kinds of native bees exist in New England.) Hummingbirds dazzle as they zero in on our lavender beebalm, hovering like tiny helicopters above the waving stalks. In late summer, the stately *cimicifuga* (called snakeroot by some, bugbane by others) boasts white flowers that tower over us, attracting at least six different varieties of native bees.

It is special to share my interest in pollinators with my grandchildren, who have studied their life cycles in school. When R was in kindergarten, his class raised monarchs in the classroom, following their development from eggs to caterpillars to emerging butterflies. The children released the monarchs onto the Boston Common in a parade, wearing monarch masks they had created.

C—who has always been fascinated by the natural world—is most curious about identification, eager to open up my butterfly chart or peruse our butterfly guidebook to pinpoint the difference between a viceroy and a monarch. This summer, she ran into the kitchen, breathless with excitement. "Nana—I've found a caterpillar on a dill plant! It's a monarch or a swallowtail." She grabbed my hand and led me to the dill patch where we knelt down to study the tiny caterpillar. The delicately striped green and gold caterpillar was perfectly camouflaged on a stalk of dill weed. I would never have noticed it myself. My friend Phyllis told me later that swallowtails like dill plants—so that answered C's question. Except for toddler J (who is scared of any six-legged creature that crawls or flies), the grandkids have become less wary of bees and understand their essential role in the garden.

For the past few years, I have focused on what I've learned about native plants as we expanded The Birdhouse gardens. From books and talks by Edward Tallamy, I learned that the trees and shrubs I had taken for granted in New England—pagoda dogwood, shad, red maple, witch hazel, red twig dogwood, sugar maple—are essential for birds and pollinators. We were thrilled to realize that the white oak we planted in my dad's memory could host more than 400 species of lepidoptera and other insects. Now, to my delight, the native Joe Pye weed lures monarchs to our garden.

Intellectually, I understand the importance of native plants, yet I can't abandon a few nonnatives that remind me of loved ones (unless they are invasive). The lilac, for instance, originated in southeastern Europe and Asia. It doesn't feed local birds or attract beneficial insects. The ancient lilacs at The Birdhouse shelter annoying pests: chipmunks, skunks, and woodchucks. This year, a mother rabbit waited beneath the lilac's branches, watching her babies slip through the woven wires of the electric fence. They mowed down my swiss chard three times, just after it sprouted—as if she'd sent them there for breakfast.

Yet my father loved lilacs. In May, the year before he died, Dad phoned me from their assisted living facility. "Take some pictures of the lilacs at our house, will you?" he asked. "They must be blooming. I need to see them again."

I heard the catch in his voice, so I hurried up their driveway. Their house sat empty and lonely on the hill, yet every lilac in their yard was in full bloom, in various shades of purple. I wept as I snapped pictures. It broke my heart to think of Dad feeling marooned, unable to be there in person. Now that my parents are gone, it's comforting that an ancient, wizened lilac blooms near their plot in the town cemetery.

On this August day, however, I'm not thinking of death. Instead, I admire a native plant that is the source of pure delight. The glittering flock of monarchs lifts and settles, gentle as feathers, on the Joe Pye weed, for one last taste before they depart. "Safe travels!" I call, as they disappear, carrying the knowledge and direction of their southbound journey inside them.

On the last day of the world
I would want to plant a tree.
—W.S. Merwin
Place

Sugar Maple

Acer saccharum

On a brisk fall day, John and I head up the steep, muddy log road to the mountain ridge we call the Saddle. Dan O'Leary—our neighbor and helper in the garden and woodlot—has spent long hours over the past few weekends mowing these former pastures with the big red International tractor that my parents bought decades ago. It's a fall ritual for us to visit the meadows after Dan has cut the chest-high weeds, allowing us to climb to the highest field and see the view.

Years before my parents purchased the property that includes the Saddle, my family hiked to these meadows for summer picnics. Back then, much of the land was still open. Dairy cows grazed in fenced pastures next to the rutted Saddle road, and the trail to a fresh spring at the edge of the forest—where we dipped metal cups into the water—was easy to find.

Originally, the two meadows—separated by a traditional stone wall—were more expansive. Even the small triangle of land, which my dad called the Saddle's pommel (and where I once spotted a black bear eating wild blackberries) was clear of trees. Now the forest has crept in around the edges and a line of poplar and maples obscures the wall. Looking north, tall trees block our former view of the Adirondacks, but the vistas to the south and west are still magnificent.

Though the meadows are above 2,000 feet—nearly inaccessible in the winter; even more so in mud season—the Saddle was once home to an active farm. Older residents, familiar with these woods and open lands, still call the first pasture "The Green Barn Meadow," in honor of an ancient barn—now long gone—that sheltered hay and cattle. Since birch and aspen have grown up to hide the stone perimeter, it takes me a few minutes to find that barn's cellar hole. I push through tangled brush to show John the old foundation. It looks tiny now.

According to retired farmers my dad interviewed years ago, the family that lived here hauled their milk to town by wagon in good weather, and by sleigh in the winter. Winters must have seemed particularly long during the days and weeks when they couldn't escape. On an earlier hike with my sons, I wondered out loud how an isolated family managed in those long, dark days. "I bet they didn't talk much," Derek said.

Now, John and I climb the steep path between the two fields. I stop to catch my breath. A brilliant fall palette of maples carpets the mountains in red, gold and orange, from the close hills to the peaks in the distance:

Dorset Mountain, Mother Myrick, and Mount Equinox. Green spruce and hemlocks darken the ridges, but maples dominate.

I have been lucky, in my life, to travel to places graced with beautiful trees. I have stood in awe in a silent grove of redwoods. On a spring trip to Japan decades ago, the cherry trees, in full bloom, were breathtaking around the temples of Kyoto. The weeping elm of my childhood—long dead to Dutch Elm disease—brings back sweet memories of the imaginary worlds we created in its shade.

But the sugar maple is my favorite tree. I love that species of maple for its sturdy, conical shape and its utility. Its golden fall foliage mimics the color of the Fancy Grade syrup made from its sap in the spring. Ancient sugar maples deep in the woods provide nesting places for wildlife, and the pileated woodpecker hammers holes to find insects hidden in its shaggy bark. Maple is easy to split and burns hot in the wood stove. Woodworkers prize the intricate patterns of spalted (curly) maple, for cabinets and high-end furniture.

My father loved maples as much as I did. When Dad learned that his close friend Peregrine was planting a forest on his farm in the Cotswolds, he somehow transported a sugar maple sapling to England (a gift that would never pass through customs now). A photo taken decades later shows Peregrine beaming next to a healthy—and large—sugar maple, labeled with its botanical sign: *acer saccharum*.

When I left the Marlboro, Vermont home where I raised my sons, I gave a final farewell to the sugar maple that stood watch over our small field near the town road, throwing my arms around it as if saying good-bye to a lover. Before our boys were born, that maple provided shade for the sheep and goats we pastured there, to eat the hardhack and scrub. As brush gave way to timothy and other grasses, we mowed the field and raked the hay into windrows by hand. Derek and Ethan helped as soon as they could manage the rakes. I remember the tick-tick of sweet sap dripping into the two buckets that we hung from that maple in sugaring season. And each time one of our sons climbed onto the yellow school bus for his first day in kindergarten, I took solace under the maple, proud yet weepy with the passage of time.

As I learned when studying field ecology many decades ago, it doesn't take long for a pasture or hayfield to revert to forest. The Saddle is a good example. If Dan didn't mow these meadows every year, old-field succession would take over. Goldenrod and milkweed would give way to shrubby plants; sun-loving birch, aspen and white pine would soon move in. After a decade or so, hardwoods would take root to join the surrounding forest.

What will the view look like, fifty years from now? As the climate warms, scientists predict that oaks will replace sugar maples. In fact, more rusty splashes of oak—their leaves clinging into November—dot the hillsides than I remember from my childhood. What will happen to the maple syrup industry? Each spring, Dan collects sap from our trees and boils it down to syrup in his saphouse. We love to stand near the roaring fire, breathing in the smell of sweet steam mixed with wood smoke. We wait for our first taste of liquid gold after he draws off finished syrup into the waiting bucket. Will the sugar maple become an oddity, an outlier? Something native to what is now Canadian tundra?

The ridgeline may hold its saddle shape, but our great-grandchildren may find a different ecosystem here—perhaps a mature forest—when they hike the trail.

As I stand in the mown field, admiring the view and listening to the rush of wind in the forest canopy, I remember a talk that John and I heard in the early days of concern about climate change, when a scientist spoke about the earth's future. In a matter-of-fact way, she told her audience that humanity might not survive if the planet's temperature continued to climb at its current rate. "The Earth will be fine," she said. "The planet will be very different—but it will continue."

She may have meant this to be reassuring. As a mother, a grandmother five times over, and as a citizen of the earth, her words broke my heart.

But perhaps my friend Phyllis Root is right—that the land *does* remember its own history. If so, are the footsteps of farmers who worked these fields embedded in the earth beneath my feet? Decades ago, men and women wrestled stones from the field, burned the stumps, and plowed deep furrows in the soil. They seeded, raked and cut sweet-smelling hay for the winter. They planted apple trees and gathered their fruit. I like to imagine that the pasture recalls the steady tread of cows headed to the barn in the evening, the creak and thump of horses pulling the hay wagon.

How about memories of our family picnics—with my parents, my brother, our aunts, uncles and cousins. Are those imprinted here? We have hiked the trail to the meadows in all seasons: once even on a pair of plodding, stubborn horses that my parents owned for a brief time. On a summer day years ago, we tried to keep up with our friend Anne's octogenarian mother, whose energy put us to shame. We have climbed the hill with Ethan, his newly pregnant wife Vita, and her mom during fall foliage season; with Derek, Ali and their girls on a winter's day; with city friends in all seasons. When my sons were young, we cajoled and played games to get them up the hill; now *their* children ride on shoulders or look for a walking stick ("like Nana's") as we hike to the top. Our youngest granddaughter, J, will be old enough to ride in a backpack to these meadows next time her family visits. She and her sisters and their cousins are the fourth generation in our family to watch the hawks catch thermals, to whine about the steep climb into the woods, then break into a run when the sky opens up and the meadow is visible at last. Will memories of the view and the hike be embedded in J's tiny bones, as they have been in mine, since childhood?

This is the Earth's garden. The limbs of ancient apple trees bend beneath the weight of their fruit. Wildlife roams freely here: we often see bear and coyote scat. Indigo buntings and scarlet tanagers flash their bright colors above the tall grass. One recent summer, Dan pointed to a wide circle of beaten grass. "A moose and her twin calves bedded down here," he said. We purposely let the field grow up each summer, to protect ground-nesting birds, and to allow monarch caterpillars to finish their cycle on the milkweed. Today, goldenrod and milkweed stems lie tangled on the ground. Milkweed seeds fly up around my boots, whirling in the wind like the monarchs that have already flown.

The men and women who originally lived at this altitude worked the land without machines. Their labor must have been backbreaking. Yet those farm families stepped outside, every morning, to witness this same view: the Taconic Mountains burnished with fall colors; the Mettawee River rushing north through the valley on its way to Canada; clouds scudding across ridges. Distant wood smoke probably twisted up from unseen chimneys then, as it does today. Redtail hawks must have soared in the valley, ancestors of the one that catches thermals below me now.

As I say goodbye to these meadows, I think about my obsession with gardens. Which garden is my true sanctuary and garden of the heart: The Last Garden I've created at The Birdhouse, in the valley—or this natural garden on the ridge, surrounded by forest, yet open to the sky?

Both.

We set off toward the path in the woods and head for home.

*Being a gardener stops you from the willing destruction of the fragile world
on which we all depend for food, health and the air we breathe.
And if gardening doesn't make you a better person,
at least it reveals the best that is in you.*
—Sydney Eddison
Gardening for a Lifetime

Daffodil

Narcissus

    It's a raw April day, threatening
snow. I kneel on the cold ground beside a bucket of uprooted daffodils,
their blooms just finished. Planting bulbs is a fall activity, but the day
before, a garden helper installed a row of Belgian blocks to define one
of our flower beds. These daffodils, planted by previous owners, pop up
in unexpected corners of the yard every spring, including along the line
where the gardener needed to set the blocks. Now the discarded bulbs fill
my bucket in a heap of faded color.

Because I inherited my father's frugal ways, and because their blooms cheered us more than usual this year, I can't bear to toss the daffodils into the compost pile. My fingers are already numb in spite of my gloves, and I haven't even begun to dig. Anyone passing by might question my sanity but of course, the road is empty. In spite of the garden helper's friendly greeting, I kept my distance when he installed the blocks. It's April of 2020.

We are barely six weeks into the isolation imposed by a growing pandemic. We have no idea that this new coronavirus will soon encircle the globe and cause millions of deaths here and abroad.

I'm planting these bulbs near the small red barn that sits on the back corner of our Birdhouse lot. The building has had many lives. When we first visited the property and opened the barn doors, we noticed an old horse stall at the back. Tooth marks gouged the wide boards of the stall where a horse must have gnawed the wood. A large iron ring was fastened to the front of the stall. A set of rickety stairs led to a hayloft, filled with wood chips and droppings from various critters. (Porcupines? Raccoons? Squirrels? All of the above?) Each spring, the maroon blossoms of a giant, wizened lilac clash with the barn's faded red siding.

Soon after we purchased The Birdhouse, we cleaned out this barn and filled it with garden tools, lawn furniture and grandkid toys. Once a tangle of day lilies, poison parsnip and blackberry vines surrounded the barn, but over the years, we have pulled out brambles and weeds. If these wilted daffodils survive, they will fill in a few bare spots.

Though a pair of bluebirds has returned to their birdhouse to raise another brood, though a male wren sings his heart out every morning outside our window at dawn, and though the days are slowly lengthening, there are few signs of spring. It's no surprise that my trowel vibrates as I stab the soil to start digging. I expect to find rocks and gravel in this unused, weedy bed. Instead, the first hole reveals wet black soil, free of stones. I clip the top of a daffodil, spoon in a few teaspoons of bone meal and compost, then settle the bulb into the dank earth. I dig another hole, then another, but find few obstructions other than the half-thawed ground itself.

I sit back on my heels. Anyone who has gardened in Vermont knows that a stone-free piece of ground is rare—if not impossible, thanks to the glaciers that once covered New England. How could this be?

Then I remember the horse stall. It's a straight shot from the back of that stall to the double doors near this bed. I picture previous owners— perhaps the daughter of the farmer who once lived here—scraping and shoveling manure into a wheelbarrow, wrestling it over the doorsill, and dumping it onto a pile beside the lilac bush. Did she return to the stall and fork fresh straw onto the clean boards? Did she take a carrot from her pocket and hold it under the horse's soft muzzle, letting its nose hairs tickle her wrist, then curry dirt and hay chaff from the mare's withers and rump? Years of hot manure must have decayed to become the fertile soil that will, hopefully, carry these bulbs into another spring.

I shiver, and not just because of the cold. Will John and I even live to see another spring? So far, the coronavirus appears to be most dangerous for people of color, for those on the front lines, and for anyone our age (we're in our seventies now). As if the earth understands the world's sorrow, this April has been the coldest ever recorded in Vermont. Icy rain has fallen many nights. Yet planting bulbs shows a stubborn belief in the future. I cover the bulbs and then, a few days later, I sow sugar snap peas and install peony hoops over the plants' first shoots.

Mother Nature is as unpredictable as ever. On May 9th, when peas poke through the black soil, and my beloved peonies are ten inches high, it *snows,* a full six inches. Heavy powder flattens my few tulips, covers the emerging daylilies, and weighs the peonies down. I rush outside to brush snow from the peony hoops. Birds mob our feeder and a male cardinal shows off his brilliant scarlet plumage against the snow—an achingly beautiful sight.

A week later, the peonies begin to push up past their hoops and the buds appear viable. Snow pea shoots uncurl, as if the snow never fell. But on June 1st, I wake at dawn to a pounding on our door. Our neighbor Dan is on our front porch. "We've had a heavy frost!" he yells. I pull on clothes and rush outside. Ice glitters across the grass. The peonies and other perennials are stiff; the frost has hardened their stems. I grab the longest hose, spraying as many of the tender plants as I can reach. I fear the worst, but three weeks later, I jot down my astonishment, in my garden journal, that the peony blooms are "as lush as I've ever seen."

When I flip through old garden journals, I realize that the garden has always been a source of comfort when times are hard. Beyond the personal losses of friends and family members, we have experienced larger tragedies: the loss of the Twin Towers; the terrorism in Boston during the Marathon bombings (which brought carnage and more explosions to our Watertown neighborhood when the bombers were caught); mass shootings so regular they form a lethal drumbeat; police killings of Black Americans across the country; and a federal administration determined to undo many of the environmental victories we worked so hard to achieve. The earth was already under assault—from climate change and drought, wars, fires and famine—before this virus arrived.

The isolation from family and friends during the pandemic shutdown has been painful. Protests in support of Black Lives Matter break out around the country, then the world; in ordinary times, we would be marching ourselves, yet fear of the virus keeps us home. With grandson R's help, we wire a BLM hashtag sign to our fence—but that's a small gesture. As I yank out a stubborn burdock, break up clods of wet soil, or lug a cartload of compost to the asparagus bed, my muscles ache. Yet the garden saves me. I'm anchored to the ground beneath my feet.

Spring gives way to summer and the garden is magnificent. John marvels at the contrast between the garden's extra beauty this year amid the escalating pandemic. Our shrubs host prolific blooms. Many perennials, taller than usual, need staking. By July, the daylilies—their buds consumed by the deer last summer—boast vibrant colors in every corner of the yard. In spite of their snowy start, the snap pea vines are heavy with pods and the fence droops beneath their weight.

When I started gardening as a young mother, my goals were practical: I wanted to feed my family and grow healthy, chemical-free food. Over the years I realized that gardening is also about technique, the layout of plants, and the nature of particular varieties. It's about warding off pests and critters, about the tools we use, the content of soil, the creation of compost, and the incorporation of organic matter. Recent studies have shown how soil, especially when enhanced by compost, retains and sequesters carbon. In this small way, our gardens help to combat climate change.

In addition to that more intellectual, practical side of gardening, I now see gardening as my commitment to the future. Since our grandchildren have been big enough to toddle into the garden, I have included them in its cycles and provided them with tools and garden gloves their size. R and K selected their pumpkin varieties from the seed catalogue this past winter, as they do every year. They usually help with the spring planting of lettuce and peas. K has the knack of spacing onion sets carefully, pointed tips up. This year, she helped me plant bean seeds as well as a packet of annuals intended to attract pollinators and it worked: bees and hummingbirds are frequent visitors and the long vines of her favorite watermelon variety snake through the perennial bed. R enjoys picking up fallen branches and loading them into the Kubota. He and John ferry them into the woods where R likes to jump out and pull the lever, dumping the tangled sticks onto our brush pile.

W and C often visit in July, when our wildflower garden is in bloom. They are old enough now to carry the clippers, cut the flowers themselves, and choose the right vases for their graceful arrangements. This year, C is especially excited about the vegetable garden. Her sharp eyes spot sugar snap peas hidden beneath their leafy vines, and new beans tucked under heart-shaped leaves. She dashes back and forth from garden to kitchen, her eyes bright as she shows me, with her hands, how much the zucchini has grown overnight. "Come see, Nana!" she exclaims. "That Better Boy tomato is almost red enough to pick!" I'm astonished. She even noticed that plant's tiny label, hidden beneath the wire hoop? I drop what I'm doing to follow her outside.

Their little sister, J, trudges to the edge of the garden and points to flowers she wants me to cut. "More," she says, pointing to an orange marigold, then a yellow nasturtium. She clutches the flowers in her small hands and jams them into a cup of water: her first flower arrangement. As she grows older, J might not remember me as an active, energetic gardener, rather as an old lady with creaky legs who grunts as she hoists herself to standing. When J was born, I was the age of my grandmothers when they had their first *great*-grandchild. Yet I still remember Frustie, my own octogenarian grandmother, stumping out to her garden, basket and clippers in hand. Hopefully I will be the same.

The grandkids are also creating gardens where they live. C and W will each have a garden at their new city home. Because of her interest in butterflies, C and I chose plants for her butterfly garden this past spring; they are already in the ground and beginning to flower. W is designing a flower bed at the front of their house. On her most recent visit, she carried pen and paper as we circled the yard, noting the names of plants. Like a mature gardener, she looked up each plant on her computer, noting whether it prefers shade or sun.

When K was about three, she told her parents that when she grew up, she planned to be "a gahdnah like Nana." Who knows if that will happen? But if the grandchildren do have their own gardens as adults, I hope these early experiences will keep them grounded in the cycle of life—and remind them of the pleasures we shared together.

I write this on a sparkling July day. Outside the bedroom alcove where I sit, a lemon-yellow daylily—called The Pride of Massachusetts—bobs in the wind, next to one aptly named Hook and Ladder, a fire engine red. Oblivious to the news of the world, the garden boasts a riot of color. I think about my grandparents, who survived the 1918 pandemic, the Great Depression and two World Wars. They kept gardening, as did my parents, my in-laws, and other gardeners from that generation. In spite of what they witnessed and experienced in those dark times, they continued to work the soil and to share their garden wisdom. I'm determined to do the same.

Half a century ago, someone —possibly a young girl—dumped manure into the spot where I dug in daffodil bulbs this April. These daffodils were, in turn, planted by the previous owner of The Birdhouse and *her* mother; decades before we embarked on our love affair with the Last Garden. My connection to gardeners of the past feels like a silken thread linking past, present and future. I hope that John and I, along with my sons and their families, will see the daffodils open on a brighter spring next year.

For the sake of the grandchildren, and for the love of all living things, I am, as Archbishop Desmond Tutu once wrote, "a prisoner of hope." As long as I can bend over to weed, clip a flower, or plant a bulb or a seed with a grandchild: I will garden.

Acknowledgments

This book would not exist if Phyllis Root and Jackie Briggs Martin—my teaching colleagues, writing collaborators and friends of the heart—hadn't provided vital inspiration, encouragement and support. Years ago, during a teaching residency at Hamline University, Phyllis gave me a copy of Terry Tempest Williams' evocative book, *When Women Were Birds*, just as I was thinking about how to tell the story of the gardens and gardeners in my life. Though Williams' stunning book is a very different kind of memoir, her book's structure inspired me to try and write in a different form.

Jackie, Phyllis and I share a passion for gardens and flowers. During many summer teaching residencies, Jackie and I rose at dawn to walk the quiet streets of St. Paul, admiring the lush, colorful gardens we passed as we talked about writing and plants. I was also lucky to join Phyllis on a few of her wildflower trips (including one cold day where we slipped and slid down an icy bank in a hopeless search for the snow trillium). Thank you, dear friends.

Thanks to other writer friends who asked, now and then, that loving question: "How's the garden memoir coming along?" Pat Lowery Collins, Kelly Easton, Elana Feldman, Jane Harwell, Karen Hesse, Gary Schmidt and Nolan Zavoral: I'm glad you prodded and cared.

In addition to the gardeners I have profiled in this story, I'm grateful to many friends and family members (including some who are gone and deeply missed) who have shared wisdom, gardening tips and plants with me over the years. Much gratitude to: Ahren Ahrenholz, Chuck Bogni; Frances Bonacci and her brothers, Joe and Sal, of Bonny's Nursery; Charlotte Burrage, Eileen Christelow, Lorni Cochran, Janet Coleman, Michael Fernandes, Judith Rivinus Fuller, Nancy Garden, Ann and Tony Gengarelly, Jane Harwell, Karen and Randy Hesse, Prosper Barter Kasrel, Tom and Polly Ketchum, Anne Koedt and Ellen Levine, Sally Macquart, Tracey Mathias, Cass Sapir, Leslie Sills, Sarah Stone, and Patty Webster.

I was blessed, in my life, to have two supportive mothers-in-law—Janet Murrow and Anne Straus. Their enthusiasm for flowers, and books about gardening, were inspiring and helpful. The members of Watertown's Friends of Bees Committee have deepened my appreciation for the intricate web that connects plants, birds and pollinators.

Special thanks to Robin Wilkerson, whose knowledge of perennials, native plants and garden designs—both wild and cultivated—is phenomenal. Her imaginative, practical garden plans have shaped our gardens, both in the city and the country.

During our years in Marlboro, Vermont, my sons, Derek and Ethan Murrow, were patient and helpful in the garden, even when they probably wished that their mother would stop pulling weeds or thinning carrots in order to kick the soccer ball around or take a hike in the woods. As they grew older, I counted on Derek, Ethan and their father to help with fencing, wedging rocks from the ground, or lugging weeds to the compost pile.

When I left the gardens of my sons' childhood, they were kind and understanding in spite of our shared heartbreak. As John and I created new gardens at the camp and then The Birdhouse, they pitched in with enthusiasm and muscle strength—and gifts of essential tools. Now, with Derek and Ethan's support, and with the encouragement of their wives, Ali and Vita, their children help me plant, tend and harvest The Birdhouse gardens each year. To my five beautiful, vibrant, helpful and playful grandchildren: May you always be blessed with lovely flowers, graceful trees and tasty veggies. I'm thrilled that you are continuing the cycle that began with your great-great-grandparents so long ago.

As my back and legs have grown weaker, I am privileged that I can rely on the physical help of younger, stronger men and women. The members of Paul Marchese's cheerful, capable crew have helped us create and maintain The Birdhouse gardens. It has been a pleasure to work alongside them, chatting about everything from politics to ticks to weeds and wildlife. When we were away from our city garden, Milson Fialho loyally stopped by to water the plants when summer's heat beat down. In Vermont, Dan O'Leary has done much of the heavy lifting, hauling manure, putting up fence and tilling soil. His deep understanding of wild creatures and their habits also helps to banish some of them—skunks, woodchucks, rabbits, fisher cats and deer—from the garden.

Thanks to Debbi Wraga, whose vision for this story never wavered, and to the dedicated staff and owners of the Northshire Bookstore, who have enriched and supported a lively community of writers and readers for decades. Thanks also to Ruth Fein Revell for her discerning eye and attention to detail. I'm especially grateful to Bobbi Angell, whose beautiful drawings illuminate the plants that inspired my memories.

Last but not least, my husband, John Straus, encourages my passion for gardening even as he works behind the scenes to do the jobs that are beyond my ability. Thanks to his quiet, steady efforts, we have an electric fence, properly wired and charged by the sun; a functioning watering system; and hooks for tools in just the right places. John has cheerfully accompanied me on countless trips to garden nurseries. His eye for color and design is a huge help. He understands, more than anyone, that working in the garden is my best therapy when times are hard, as well as a continuous source of pleasure and fulfillment. For this writer, there are no words strong enough to express my gratitude and love to my dearest gardening companion.

About The Illustrator
Bobbi Angell

Botanical and scientific artist Bobbi Angell draws plants at her home in southern Vermont where she gardens, searches for native flowers, illustrates books and works on copper etchings.

Visit her website: www.bobbiangell.com

About The Author
Liza Ketchum

Liza Ketchum is the award-winning author of seventeen books of fiction and non-fiction for young readers. Her historical novels include two with Vermont connections: *The Life Fantastic*, a vaudeville story from 1913; and *Where the Great Hawk Flies*, winner of the Massachusetts Book Award for Young Adults. An ardent baseball fan, Liza's most recent contemporary novel, *Out of Left Field*, takes place during the Red Sox winning season of 2004. She is a co-author, with Phyllis Root and Jackie Briggs Martin, of the forthcoming *Begin With a Bee*, a non-fiction picture book illustrated by Claudia McGehee. Learn more at her website: www.lizaketchum.org

A citizen scientist volunteer and climate activist, Liza enjoys writing essays on issues related to gardening, the environment, and climate change. Founder of the Meetinghouse School in Marlboro, Vermont— where she raised her two sons—she taught creative writing at the graduate level at Hamline University in St. Paul, at Rhode Island College's ASTAL Institute, at Emerson College, Simmons College, and Vermont College of Fine Arts. She and her husband divide their time between Massachusetts and Vermont.

The Last Garden
A Memoir

ISBN Number: 978-1-60571-518-6

Printed in the United States of America

Other Books by Liza Ketchum:

Young Adult Fiction
Out of Left Field
Fire In the Heart
Twelve Days in August
Blue Coyote

Middle Grade Fiction
Allergic to My Family
The Ghost of Lost Island
Dancing on the Table

Historical Fiction
The Life Fantastic
Newsgirl
Where the Great Hawk Flies
West Against the Wind
Orphan Journey Home

True Stories
Into a New Country: Eight Remarkable Women of the West
The Gold Rush

Picture Book
Begin With a Bee: Co-authors: Jackie Briggs Martin and Phyllis Root.
Illustrated by Claudia McGehee

SHIRES PRESS
P.O. Box 2200 | Manchester Center, VT 05255 | www.northshire.com

CPSIA information can be obtained
at www.ICGtesting.com
Printed in the USA
LVHW072310070521
686824LV00001B/3